MW00377952

Babe and Kris Winkelman's

ULTIMATE WILD GAME AND FISH COOKBOOK

Foreword

I grew up believing you don't kill anything you don't plan to eat. That's why I've worked so hard to develop recipes the entire family can enjoy. The job starts with proper care and handling of the meat from the field or lake to the freezer. When sportsmen complain that their walleye tastes "fishy" or their venison "smells funny", I usually suspect it's because they didn't give adequate attention to the cleaning, transporting, packaging and freezing of the game.

Preparing the game is the next step. Wild game is, by nature, leaner than domestic meat, and that means it must be prepared differently. The recipes in this cookbook are designed to yield moist, flavorful dishes without sacrificing the distinctive flavor of the game.

It's my sincere hope that your family will enjoy the recipes in this cookbook as much as Babe, Karlee and I have enjoyed them.

Kris Winkelman

Text © 2001 Babe Winkelman Productions
Photographs © Dan Nelson
Michael Aulie, Sothers Photography

All rights reserved. No portion of this book may be reproduced in any manner without written permission from Babe Winkelman Productions.

Editor: Dan Nelson
Cover and Book Design: Nelson Graphic Design & Advertising
Written by: Kris Winkelman, Dan Nelson
Production Assistant: Nate Berg
ISBN 0-915405-10-5

Additional copies available for $19.95 plus $4.50 shipping and handling from:
Babe Winkelman Productions, PO Box 407, Brainerd, Minnesota 56401
For more Kris Winkelman recipes, log on to www.winkelman.com
Printed in USA

Table of Contents

Acknowledgements

A great many people—too many to mention them all by name—contributed in one way or another to the writing of this cookbook. First, I want to pass along a special thanks to all the television viewers for their words of encouragement over the years. Without your letters and emails, this project may never have been undertaken.

A special thanks to my good friends Chris Gerard, Elaine Compton and Teresa Martin who helped out in the kitchen, searched for recipes to test and provided their all-important encouragement and support.

My sister Sue Petersen was an active participant in the writing of this cookbook. Together we spent countless hours experimenting with different recipes. Not all of them turned out, but even when the recipes weren't the best we always had fun trying.

My brother Ron Pechstein also contributed some of his favorite family recipes, many of which we've been enjoying for years.

I'd also like to thank Dan Nelson, who compiled the recipes, put them into words and pulled the whole cookbook project together. Dan and I spent many days in the kitchen, trying different recipes and shooting some of the photographs found in the book.

A special thanks to my daughter Karlee for being so understanding of the time it takes to make a cookbook and for being Mom's little helper.

A very special thanks to my husband Babe for believing in me. It's one thing to whip up dishes for friends and family; it's entirely something else again to share those dishes with the public on Babe's television shows and in a cookbook. Without Babe's faith and constant encouragement, this book never would have been published. Finally, I'd like to recognize my parents, Gladys and Carl Pechstein for instilling in me an appreciation for the outdoors and its endless bounty.

Introduction

A wise man said happiness isn't a destination, it's a journey. This cookbook is dedicated to the millions of hunters and fishermen who understand that tagging a deer or collecting a limit of fish isn't the end of the journey, it's only the beginning.

This book was written for those outdoor aficionados who have discovered that transforming a bag of frozen venison into a gourmet meal can be every bit as challenging and rewarding as bagging the deer; who experiment with recipes as enthusiastically as they seek out new fishing holes.

It is not the goal of this cookbook to turn sportsmen into French chefs, nor is it our intention to pass along "grandma's favorite game recipes". Grandma's venison and duck were so dry and chewy they were barely edible; chefs prepare pen-raised, fattened game more akin to aged beef than wild venison. The game in our freezers requires a different approach, and in preparing this reference we've searched for techniques that bring out the best in the wild harvest.

The decision to write this book was easy. Ever since I started the "Kris' Kitchen" feature on Babe's **Good Fishing** and **Outdoor Secrets** television shows, I've literally been overwhelmed with letters, emails and phone calls from viewers requesting a game and fish cookbook. Eating wild game, it seems, has become an obsession with the country's 50 million anglers and 16 million hunters.

I'm guessing this growing passion for outdoor cuisine has a lot to do with demographics. The average sportsman is around 50 years of age and has been enjoying the outdoors for 40 years. As the sporting public matures, individuals tend to be less concerned about trophies and limits and more focused on the total experience. For many of us, preparing and eating the game and fish we collect has become a big part of that experience.

The growing popularity of game in restaurants has been another factor. Dishes like venison medallions, roast Long Island Duckling, braised pheasant and baked walleye are showing up on the menus of fine dining establishments everywhere. Eating gourmet dishes prepared by qualified chefs taught us that venison doesn't have to taste like liver and duck needn't be as dry and flavorless as a loaf of week-old bread.

Admittedly the venison and duck served in restaurants isn't the same as the game we bring home from our weekend outings. It's pen-raised, fattened and, in the case of Long Island duckling, isn't even the same species. On the other hand, if the chefs at those restaurants over-cooked game the way many sportsmen prepare it, the final product would be as dry, tough and disagreeable as the venison fixed in kitchens across the country every day.

The goal of many home cooks is to make venison taste like beef and pheasant taste like chicken. That's a mistake, because wild game has a rich, distinct flavor all its own, a flavor meant to be accentuated, not masked.

Those who have uncovered the secrets to preparing wild game often find they enjoy venison more than beef and prefer pheasant, quail and ruffed grouse to chicken.

I'm not a trained chef, but when you're married to Babe Winkelman—a man whose appetite for hunting and fishing is exceeded only by his appetite for eating game—you learn your way around the kitchen in a hurry.

The goal of this cookbook was to find a happy middle ground between the complicated recipes utilizing hard-to-find ingredients used by professional chefs and the smother-it-in-cream-of-mushroom-soup recipes most of us grew up with.

Many of the meals require a bit more preparation time. After all, no one expects to take a deer in 15 minutes, why would anyone think they could slap together a delicious meal that quickly? But we've also included a number of quick and easy recipes for cooks on the go.

Some of the recipes in this cookbook were provided by friends and acquaintances across the continent. We started picking up recipes at the lodges we visited in the making of our *Good Fishing* and *Outdoors Secrets* television shows. Hunting and fishing companions chipped in their favorite dishes, as did dinner guests at our home.

We watched television cooking shows, studied cookbooks and scoured the internet for recipe ideas. Most of the recipes we found—fully three-fourths of them—simply didn't work on wild game. Of the rest, nearly all had to be tweaked in one way or another.

Along the way we discovered that getting there is, indeed, half the fun. The countless days we've spent in the kitchen developing recipes have been every bit as enjoyable as the days devoted to collecting that game.

Every serious hunter or fisherman knows what it's like to watch a glorious sunset at the end of a special day in the field or on the water. Who among us hasn't toasted such a day with, "It's Miller time," or "Here's to great days with special friends".

Fortunately, those memorable outings don't have to end at sunset. After the rods and guns have been put away, grilling a venison steak or frying up a batch of crappie is the perfect way to relive those wonderful days afield.

That lesson certainly hasn't been lost on Bob Musil, executive director of the Red Wing (Minnesota) Convention and Visitor's Bureau. Bob sent along a recipe for baked pheasant with asparagus and bleu cheese which began, "Uncork a bottle of white wine and pour yourself a glass, taking care to reserve at least ¼ cup for the recipe." After putting the dish in the oven, he suggests, "Pour yourself another glass of wine, you deserve it." Finally, he says to cook the dish "…approximately 50 minutes or until sauce is bubbly and wine is gone."

And that, folks, is the right approach to preparing game and fish. Take your time, do it right, savor the moment and most of all, "enjoy".

Babe's Introduction

Those who know me may wonder why I'm listed as co-author of this cookbook. After all, everyone knows it's Kris—not me—who does most of the cooking in our house.

On the other hand, I believe that preparing game and fish should be a family activity. Sharing in the preparation and enjoyment of nature's bounty is an important part of the outdoor experience, and I hope that lending my name to the book will encourage other sportsmen to get involved in the process.

Some of our sponsors say it's women—not men—who do all the cooking. I don't believe that. I know a lot of men who enjoy preparing game and fish, just as I know a lot of women who enjoy hunting and fishing.

Kris is one of those women. She's been with me on dozens of hunting and fishing trips. She's taken trophy mule deer, bagged limits of pheasants and partridge and caught some monster fish.

When it comes to the outdoors, there is no division of chores. Gone are the days when men bring home the meat and women fix it. Women are joining the ranks of hunters and fishers faster than any other segment of the population, and I think that's great. An increasing number of men can be found grilling venison steaks or frying up a batch of fish fillets, and I think that's great, too.

I'm convinced that outdoor cuisine and outdoor adventure are best shared with family, and I'm glad Kris feels the same. It's my hope that lending my name to this cookbook will convince other sportsmen to put on an apron and step into the kitchen.

I encourage men and women to take at least one night a week to experiment with a new fish or game recipe. Make a night of it. Pop the cork on a bottle of wine, try one of the recipes from this book and re-live your adventures in the great outdoors with family and friends.

It's a wonderful way to spend an evening.

Stocks

Taking Stock
The Foundation of the Kitchen

What do professional chefs know that the rest of us don't? Why are the venison, duck and pheasant served in fine restaurants so moist, tender and flavorful?

For one thing, the game prepared in professional kitchens is raised commercially and is "fed" so it has more fat (juice) and a milder flavor than its wild cousins. But that's only part of the answer. Any good chef could take game from your freezer and turn it into a meal fit for a king. So what's their secret?

Aside from the fact that they're trained chefs, the "secret" ingredient found in most professional kitchens is the stocks used in preparing soups and braising, poaching or stewing the meat. These homemade stocks also are the foundation for the delicious sauces that accompany most meals.

The French term for stock is Fonds de Cuisine, which translates into "the foundation of the kitchen".

Stock is made by simmering the bones and meat of birds or animals along with vegetables and seasonings called a bouquet garni. Of all the chefs I've interviewed over the years, every one has confessed that a well-tended stock is the heart and soul of wild-game cookery.

If there's one thing I learned in preparing this cookbook it's that braising, stewing or poaching meat in the appropriate stock produces the moistest, most flavorful dishes imaginable, and those same stocks can be used to make wonderful sauces and gravies that further accentuate the flavor of the dish. I use stock rather than water to boil wild rice, steam vegetables and moisten stuffing, all with exceptional results.

If stocks are the "secret ingredient" in wild-game cookery, they must be difficult to make, right? Actually stocks are very simple to prepare, requiring little more than peeling a few vegetables and occasionally skimming the froth from the surface early in the simmering process. A finished stock can be frozen for months and thawed whenever you plan to make a special dish.

Doesn't canned chicken broth or beef broth produce the same results? While store-bought broth will work, it doesn't have the flavor or richness of homemade stock. Besides, using a canned chicken broth will lend a chicken flavor to your pheasant, grouse or quail.

In a pinch, it's possible to enhance a canned broth, and that's a technique we'll review in this section. Preparing stocks also is a great way to utilize those parts of the game that might normally go to waste. Leg, shank or shoulder bones of a deer that would normally be discarded are perfect for making stock. Upland bird hunters who typically breast their game can use the carcass to prepare a delicious stock. Sportsmen who've been looking for a way to utilize the legs of game birds need look no further. All these "spare parts" can be frozen until the day you decide to make stock.

If you really want to stretch your food budget, it's possible to pick the meat from the bones while it still has a little flavor and use it in another recipe. For example, you can salvage enough meat from two pheasant carcasses to fix such delicious dishes as "pheasant pot pie" or "pheasant and dumplings".

When visiting the meat department of your favorite grocery store, watch for sales on chicken legs and inexpensive cuts of meat or soup bones. Put them in the freezer and add them to the pot next time you simmer up a fresh batch of stock. If you serve chicken or turkey, save the carcass in a Ziploc bag in the freezer.

Preparing a good stock usually takes only a few hours, and during most of that time it just sits there and simmers. Once you've cut up the vegetables and skimmed a bit of froth, it's a hands-off operation.

Many of the recipes in this cookbook call for "game stock" or "venison stock". If you don't have them, you can substitute chicken broth or beef broth, but I suspect you'd be far more satisfied with the results if you used homemade stock or, at the very least, enhanced stock.

Do's and Don'ts of Stock-Making

- Always use cold water and heat it very slowly.
- Never allow the water to boil
- Use only enough water to cover the bones. Add water to replace evaporation.
- During the first hour or so, carefully skim the froth from the surface
- Don't touch or stir the ingredients during simmering.
- Never cover the stockpot.
- When straining at the end, don't press vegetables. Rather, allow them to drain naturally.
- Allow the strained stock to cool, preferably in a sink of ice, then refrigerate. Stock is a perfect medium for bacteria, so don't allow it to sit around at room temperature for long.
- Store stock 3 to 4 days, covered, in a refrigerator. If you need to store it longer than that, bring it to a simmer, skim and return to the refrigerator for another 3 to 4 days.

Brown Gamebird Stock

Preheat the oven to 400 degrees

Thoroughly wash the carcasses of two or three upland game birds or waterfowl and separate the wings, breast, back and thighs. Carefully cut away any excess fat. Place the pieces in the bottom of a large roasting pan and place in the oven for 45 minutes to 1 hour, or until the pieces are completely browned. Using a tong, turn the pieces occasionally to ensure even browning. Once the pieces are browned, add to the roaster:

1 medium onion, coarsely chopped
2 carrot, coarsely chopped
1 celery stalk, coarsely chopped

Allow the vegetables to brown, stirring often. Once the vegetables have browned, place meat and vegetables into a large stockpot. Place the roaster on a burner over high heat and add a quart of water. When the pan gets hot, deglaze by scraping the caramelized bits off the bottom of the pan with a wooden spoon. Add the dark-colored water to the stockpot. Add enough water to cover the bird parts and bring the stockpot to a simmer—do not boil. During the first 45 minutes, skim any froth that appears on the surface with a spoon or ladle to remove any fat. After about 45 minutes, add:

a bouquet garni (2 bay leaves, parsley, 10 whole peppercorns, parsley flakes, thyme, 1 large clove of crushed garlic, all wrapped and tied in a piece of cheesecloth.)

Cook the stock for 3 hours uncovered. Strain the stock through a wire strainer lined with cheesecloth and cool at room temperature. Refrigerate overnight. The next day, strain the stock again, discarding the fat that congealed on the surface.

Put the finished stock in Ziploc two- and 3-cup containers and place in the freezer.
Be sure to mark the lid with the type of stock in those containers.

White Gamebird Stock

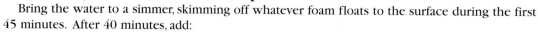

In a large stockpot, combine:

Bird carcasses, cut into pieces
1 medium onion, coarsely chopped
1 carrot, coarsely chopped
1 celery stalk, coarsely chopped
enough cold water to cover bird parts

Bring the water to a simmer, skimming off whatever foam floats to the surface during the first 45 minutes. After 40 minutes, add:

a bouquet garni (2 bay leaves, parsley flakes, thyme, 10 whole peppercorns, 1 large clove of sliced garlic, all wrapped and tied in a piece of cheesecloth.)

Simmer, uncovered, for 3 hours. Strain, cool, refrigerate and strain again as in the brown stock.

Venison Stock

Preheat oven to 400 degrees.

Place meat—preferably bones with meat—in roaster pan and place in the oven for 45 minutes or until brown. When the bones have browned, add:

1 medium onion, coarsely chopped
2 carrots, coarsely chopped
2 celery stalks, coarsely chopped

Return roasting pan to the oven and continue to bake until the vegetables are brown. When the vegetables are browned, place meat and vegetables in a stockpot and cover nearly to the top with water.

Place roaster on a burner over high heat and deglaze by pouring in 2 cups of water and stirring the caramelized bits off the bottom. Add the dark water to the stockpot and bring to a simmer, skimming off any fat that accumulates on the surface during the first hour. Add a bouquet garni (see above) and continue to simmer for another 5 hours. Stain, discarding bones and vegetables, cool and refrigerate as in the gamebird stock above.

Pressure Cooker Stocks

Gamebird Stock

Game cooks who feel they don't have time to tend a stock for several hours might want to consider using a pressure cooker. It takes a lot less time and still produces a great stock.

To the bottom of the pressure cooker over medium-high heat, add:

1 tablespoon of vegetable oil

Cut two or three gamebird carcasses into pieces and brown them in the cooker. Remove the bird pieces to a plate, remove any fat that may have accumulated and add and brown:

1 medium onion, coarsely chopped
1 medium carrot, coarsely chopped
1 celery stalk, coarsely chopped

When the vegetables have softened and browned, deglaze the bottom of the pan by adding, over high heat:

2 cups of water

Scrap up the browned bits and return the bird pieces and vegetables to the cooker, adding:

2 quarts of water
thyme
6 whole peppercorns
parsley
2 bay leaves
1 large clove of garlic, chopped

Lock the lid in place and set the burner on high at 15 pounds of pressure. Once the cooker is up to heat, adjust the heat to maintain the pressure (see manufacturer's recommendations) and cook for 20 minutes. Release the pressure and remove the lid, allowing the stock to simmer for an additional hour before straining, refrigerating and freezing.

Venison Stock

Over medium-high heat, add to the pressure cooker:

1 tablespoon vegetable oil

Add and brown thoroughly:

3 to 4 pounds of venison bones (with some meat)

Remove the meat and set aside. Add and brown:

1 medium onion, coarsely chopped
1 carrot, coarsely chopped
1 celery stalk, coarsely chopped
1 large clove of garlic, coarsely chopped

Cook, stirring, until the vegetables are browned. Next, deglaze the cooker by stirring in, over high heat:

2 cups of water

When the caramelized bits have been scraped into the water, put into the cooker:

The meat
10 whole peppercorns
thyme
parsley
2 bay leaves
2 quarts of water

When the pressure cooker is up to heat, adjust the temperature according to the manufacturer's recommendations and cook at 15 pounds of pressure for 20 minutes. Remove lid and allow to simmer for an additional hour. Strain, refrigerate and freeze as in previous recipes.

Fish Stock

Making a fish stock is easier than you might think. A good homemade stock not only is an important ingredient in a number of delicious sauces, it also makes for a wonderful poaching liquid.

Before making the stock, be sure to remove the gills, skin, fins, tail and stomach lining from the fish. You just want the heads, bones and whatever meat was left after cleaning.
Combine in a large stockpot:

2 pounds of fish frames
1 onion, thinly sliced
1 teaspoon lemon juice
1 cup dry white wine
half a dozen fresh parsley stems (optional; not the leaves)
salt
enough cold water to cover the frames

Simmer uncovered for 30 minutes. Strain and allow to cool at room temperature. Refrigerate and strain again through cheesecloth.
I like to freeze the stock in reusable Ziploc plastic containers (always label stocks).

Emergency Fish Stock

If a sauce recipe calls for a fish stock and you have none, you can always make an "emergency" stock. This quick-and-easy stock tastes almost as good as the real thing. Bottled clam juice—the key ingredient—is available at most grocery stores.

In a saucepan, combine:

1 ½ cup bottled clam juice
1 cup water
1 cup dry white wine
1 onion, thinly sliced
half a dozen parsley stems (no leaves)

Simmer 30 minutes, strain through cheesecloth and cool. Use within two days.

Cooking Basics

Clarified Butter: Clarified butter is used in a number of recipes in this cookbook because it burns less easily than regular butter. To clarify butter, melt the butter over very low heat and gently pour it into a clear measuring cup and place in the refrigerator. When the butter hardens, scrape off the foam from the top. Place the cup in the microwave and melt it again. What remains will be a milky residue on the bottom and a clear yellow liquid on top. Strain the butter, saving the clear yellow liquid and discarding the milky particles on the bottom.

Roux: A roux is a thickening agent used in sauces and gravies. In most cases, we prefer it to cornstarch or other thickeners. It's easy to make and can be stored in the refrigerator or freezer in Ziploc plastic containers. I always have a cup or two in the refrigerator ready to use. To prepare a roux, melt butter in a saucepan and stir in an equal amount of flour, stirring until the flour is completely blended and the roux takes on a nutty aroma.

Most cooks use a white or blonde roux, which takes only minutes to prepare. For dark sauces, a dark roux can be prepared by cooking the roux longer until the roux becomes darker. Some chefs recommend putting the roux in a 375-degree oven for 1 hour, stirring occasionally. The finished produce will be very dark in color and have the consistency of sand.

Cornstarch: If cornstarch is used as a thickening agent, mix a small amount of cornstarch in cold water, mixing thoroughly. Mixing cornstarch in wine is perhaps a better alternative. Whichever liquid is used, be certain the cornstarch is thoroughly dissolved in the liquid before adding to the gravy, sauce or whatever is to be thickened.

Bread Crumbs: Some of the recipes in this cookbook call for bread crumbs. Making your own not only is less expensive than purchasing prepared crumbs, it also produces a more flavorful product. To make bread-crumbs, simply cut the crust off fresh bread and process in a blender or a food processor a few slices at a time.

Roasted Garlic: If a recipe calls for roasted garlic, cut off the top of an unpeeled head of garlic, rub the head with olive oil and place in a 350-degree oven in a baking dish or piece of tinfoil for one hour. Remove from the oven, and when the garlic is cool enough to handle, separate the cloves and squeeze (using a garlic press or by pressing the side of a large knife) the juice and pulp from the clove.

Bouquet Garni: A bouquet garni can be used to flavor stocks, sauces or soups while keeping the seasonings from becoming part of the dish. In a small piece of cheesecloth, place two small bay leaves, some fresh chopped (or dried) parsley, 1 teaspoon of dried thyme, 10 whole black peppercorns and a large clove of crushed garlic. Tie the cheesecloth with a piece of string and discard when the cooking is completed.

Deglazing a pan: As meats are being cooked or browned they give off flavorful juices that form as caramelized bits on the bottom of the sauté pan. Deglazing is a method of incorporating the flavor of these juices into the dish, stock or sauce that accompanies it. When the meat has been removed from the pan, a small amount of water, wine, liquor or stock is added to the hot pan and stirred until the accumulated bits have been dissolved into the liquid.

Crème fraiche: Most restaurants use a double cream or crème fraiche rather than the heavy cream available in grocery stores. Crème fraiche has a nutty flavor and can be boiled without curdling. Crème fraiche is simple to make. Stir 1 tablespoon of buttermilk into 1 cup of heavy cream and heat, stirring, over very low heat (not more than 85 degrees). Let the mixture stand at room temperature, loosely covered. The cream will thicken, usually within 5 to 8 hours. It can be stored in the refrigerator up to 10 days.

Fall-Off-The-Bone Venison Pot Roast

20

Fall-Off-The-Bone Venison Pot Roast

Preheat the oven to 300 degrees. Cut away all the silver skin and season the roast liberally with Montreal steak seasoning. Place a large, heavy-bottomed Dutch oven (with a tight-sealing lid) on the stove over medium-high heat and coat the bottom with:

2 tablespoons of vegetable oil

When the oil is hot, place the roast in the Dutch oven and completely brown on all sides. Browning seals in the juices. Taking a little extra time to make sure the sides and ends are seared is worth the effort. When the roast is properly seared, remove the Dutch oven from the burner and drain any excess oil. Return to the burner and add, bringing to a boil:

2 cups of white onions, chopped	**1 large tomato, cored and sliced**
3 bay leaves	**1 teaspoon of dried thyme**
2 cups of white wine	**½ cup of dark venison stock**

Once the liquid comes to a full boil, cover the Dutch oven and place in the oven for 4 hours.

Next, strain the liquid and discard the vegetables and bay leaves, squeezing the liquid from the vegetables using a wooden spoon. Pour the liquid back into the Dutch oven and add:

1 pound of baby carrots (or regular carrots peeled and cut)
1 pound of baby red potatoes, (peeled and cut in half)
½ pound small white onions

Place the oven on the burner and bring the liquid to a boil. Once it comes to a boil, cover and return to the 300-degree oven for and hour or until the vegetables are soft. Use a slotted spoon to remove the vegetables from the liquid and place in a covered bowl. Place the Dutch oven on the burner at medium heat. When it comes to a boil, thicken the gravy by stirring in a mixture of:

2 tablespoons white wine	**2 tablespoons cornstarch**

Use only enough of the cornstarch mixture to thicken the gravy. Season to taste with:

Salt and pepper	**Chopped parsley**

Barbecue Venison

I've tried a lot of barbecue recipes and this is one of the best. It works very well for ribs, but is also great with steaks and chops. You can make this dish using a commercial barbecue sauce, but it isn't as tasty as the homemade version.

Preheat oven to 250 degrees
In a large non-stick skillet or roasting pan, combine:

Meat (ribs, steaks or chops)
2 cups homemade venison stock (beef broth is optional)
1 onion, sliced
2 bay leaves
half a dozen whole black peppercorns
salt and pepper

Bring the broth to a boil for 5 minutes, then cover and place in the oven

To prepare the sauce:
Combine is a skillet and bring to a rapid boil, stirring constantly:

2 cups ketchup   **1 cup cider vinegar**
2 cloves garlic, minced   **¼ cup soy sauce**
¼ cup Worcestershire sauce   **¾ cup honey**
8 ounces pineapple juice (fresh or canned)
1 teaspoon dried oregano   **1 teaspoon dried thyme**
½ teaspoon crushed red pepper

Reduce heat and cook for 1 hour, stirring occasionally.
Preheat charcoal or gas grill. Coat the ribs thoroughly with the sauce and finish on the grill. I prefer to serve this meal with one of the squash-potato or sweet potato-potato side dishes. You'll find several in the side-dish section of the cookbook.

Jim Zumbo's Ginger Elk

This recipe was provided by our friend Jim Zumbo, who is not only one of the great outdoor writers in the country but a wonderful wild-game cook to boot.

Slice, against the grain:
> **1 pound of elk steak**

Place the slices in a Ziploc bag and add:
> **2 onions, sliced**
> **2 cloves garlic**
> **⅓ cup minced ginger root**

Combine and add to Ziploc:
> **1 teaspoon sugar**
> **¾ cup soy sauce**

Shake and seal the bag, placing in the refrigerator for 1 hour.

Brown in oil:
> **6 slices of ginger root**

Remove pan from stove and discard ginger slices.

Drain most of the soy sauce from the marinade, place meat in a hot skillet and sauté. Sprinkle over the top of the meat:
> **2 tablespoons of cornstarch**

Sauté for a few more minutes, stirring constantly.

23

Bacon-Wrapped Backstrap with Blackberry Sauce

Don't be deceived by the long name, this dish is easy and quick.
The sauce takes a few minutes to prepare, but it's worth the effort.

Preheat oven to 350 degrees
Season with salt, pepper and Montreal steak seasoning:
   2 pounds of venison backstrap
Wrap the meat completely with:
   thin slices of bacon
Place in the oven in a glass baking dish, uncovered, until cooked to the desired doneness

To prepare the sauce:
Heat in a saucepan over medium heat:
   1 tablespoon olive oil
Add and cook until soft and slightly browned:
   ¼ cup finely chopped shallots
Increase heat and add, boiling until reduced by half:
   2 cups red wine (Merlot, cabernet sauvignon or
   pinot noir all work well)

Add and continue to boil until reduced to the desired consistency:
   3 cups game stock (or beef broth)
   2 cup frozen blackberries (fresh if available)
   a pinch of dried sage

The sauce doesn't have to reduce to a syrup-like consistency. It can be a bit on the runny side. When the sauce is ready, strain it through a sieve, pressing the blackberry juice to save all the liquid. Salt and pepper to taste.

Pour small amounts of the sauce on the plate, slice the backstrap diagonally and place several pieces over the sauce.
Serve with your favorite wild rice dish or mixed vegetables and a glass of hearty red wine.

Venison Meat Balls

Looking for a great recipe for that ground venison in your freezer?
You'll like this one. It works with any kind of ground venison.

In a heavy-bottomed skillet, melt:
> **1 tablespoon butter**

Add and cook until soft:
> **1 tablespoon minced onions**

Set aside. In a large bowl, blend with an electric mixer:
> **1 cup fresh bread crumbs**
> **1 cup water**

Add the onions and:
> **1 ½ pound ground venison**
> **½ pound ground pork**
> **2 large egg yolks**
> **salt and fresh ground pepper to taste**
> **¼ teaspoon seasoning salt**

Blend at low speed until thoroughly mixed. Using a rounded spoon, form meat mixture into small balls and brown in a large skillet with:
> **2 tablespoons melted butter**

When done, remove the meat balls to a platter and add to the skillet and bring to a simmer:
> **2 cups venison stock (beef broth will also work)**

When the stock is simmering stir in a little bit at a time until the gravy thickens:
> **Dark roux**

When the gravy is thick, reduce the heat to low, place the meatballs in the gravy and cover until ready to be served.

Serve with garlic mashed potatoes.

Venison Chislic

Big Game Chislic

In all my travels, I've only run across a dish called "chislic" in South Dakota. Chislic is nothing more than deep-fried chunks of meat, and it's found on the appetizer menus of bars and restaurants all across the state. I decided to give it a try with venison and it was a big hit. It can be prepared with any big game and it takes only seconds to make.

Start by cutting into bite-sized chunks:
>**1 pound venison steak or roast**

Next, marinate the chunks for at least an hour in:
>**Teriyaki sauce (or your favorite marinade)**

Finally, deep-fry the chunks in:
>**Vegetable oil or canola oil**

Place on a paper towel to absorb the excess grease and serve with barbecue sauce or your favorite dipping sauce

Governor's Venison Recipe

Jesse Ventura, the governor of Minnesota, once told an interviewer that one of the biggest perks of his job was having his own chefs. Because Minnesota is such an outdoor state, we figured those chefs might have some good game and fish recipes, and we were right. Chef Ken Grogg provided several recipes for this cookbook, including this one for "venison forestiere". We tried it and liked it. We think you will, too.

Preheat oven to 350 degrees.
Season with salt and pepper and brown in olive oil:

3 pounds of venison

Remove the venison, and add to the pan drippings:

2 tablespoons of butter   **3 sprigs of thyme**
2 shallots, finely diced   **2 cloves of garlic, crushed**
3 cups of mushrooms, chopped

When the mushrooms have softened, remove from the skillet and de-glaze with:

¼ cup brandy

Flame the brandy, then add:

¼ cup red wine

In a saucepan, bring to a boil:

3 cups venison stock (or beef broth)

Add the brandy/wine sauce to the stock and reduce to the desired consistency
Place the venison on a cookie sheet and place in the oven for 10 minutes
to finish cooking. Return the mushrooms to the sauce and season
with salt and pepper. Allow the venison to rest on a warm plate,
slice and pour the sauce over the slices.

Finger-Licking Honey-Glazed Venison Ribs

I'm betting this will quickly become a family favorite, even for folks who don't think they like venison ribs. It's fairly easy to make and works with deer, elk, moose or any big-game animal. The key to this recipe is slow-cooking the ribs in a hearty venison stock, which is easy to make. If you don't have the bones to make a home-made stock, reduced beef broth will work.

For the marinade:
In a small sauce pan, combine over moderate heat:

3 cloves garlic, sliced	**1 cup brown sugar**
1 cup honey	**¼ cup white wine vinegar**
¼ cup Worcestershire sauce	**Juice of one orange**
1 tablespoon salt	**1 tablespoon pepper**

Allow marinade to cool. Next, place ribs in a gallon-sized Slide-Loc bags, pour marinade into bags, squeeze out the air and allow the bags to cool in refrigerator for up to 24 hours.

To prepare the ribs:
Preheat oven to 400 degrees.

Remove ribs from plastic bags, reserving the marinade. Place ribs in a large roasting pan and place in the center of the oven, meat-side down. Allow the ribs to brown, about 15 minutes on each side. When the ribs are browned, turn the oven down to 200 degrees and remove roasting pan from oven. Place ribs on a platter and place roasting pan on hot burner. Pour in half a cup of stock and scrape up the caramelized bits using a spatula or wooden spoon.

Remove from burner, mix in 2 more cups of stock and put ribs back in the roasting pan. Cover and place in the 200-degree oven for 2 hours.

Just before the ribs are done, pour the marinade in a saucepan and heat until it reduces and thickens. Remove the ribs from the oven, discard the stock and baste the ribs liberally with the thickened marinade. Heat oven to 300 degrees. Continue to baste every 15 minutes for 1 hour.

Before serving, heat the remaining marinade and pour over the ribs.

Butt Kick'n Barbeque

"I normally don't like cover sauces that eliminate the uniqueness of game meat, but this is a great way to prepare any kind of game."
So wrote Randy Schoeck of archery-maker Easton, who provided this recipe which he calls Butt Kick'n Barbeque.

Start by combining in a large skillet:

2 pounds of cubed venison (moose, elk, deer, caribou)
olive oil   **salt and pepper**

In a Dutch oven or heavy skillet, combine and heat until smooth:

1 cup ketchup   **⅓ cup red-wine vinegar**
¼ cup Worcestershire sauce   **1 large onion, diced**
3 cloves garlic, minced   **2 Jalapeno peppers, minced**

When the sauce is smooth, slowly stir in:

¾ cup brown sugar

Add the browned meat, cover and simmer for an hour "until everything is nice and friendly in the pot."

Randy suggests serving over rice, noodles or slabs of bread. He says "cold, cold beer is a must!"

Spiced Elk Heart

When we asked different conservation organizations to contribute recipes, we didn't expect to receive one for "spiced elk heart", but that's what we got from our friends at the Rocky Mountain Elk Foundation (RMEF) in Montana. They swear it's not only unique, but delicious as well. This recipe was provided by RMEF by Suzette Horton of Idaho Falls, ID.

In a crock pot, place:

1 elk heart   **4 cups hot water**
⅓ cup vinegar   **3 tablespoons sugar**
2 teaspoons salt   **3 bay leaves**
18 whole cloves   **¾ cup onion, sliced**
1 tablespoon lemon zest (grated lemon peel)

Cook for 12 hours and serve either hot or cold.

Snowbank Italian Game Roast

It's not often anyone has to serve wild game for 50 guests, but that's exactly the predicament I found myself facing at our last office Christmas party. Because we're an outdoor company, I wanted to serve lots of game dishes. But there's only so much space in the oven and just a limited amount of time the day of the party. The solution? I actually made seven different roasts two days ahead of time in a large electric roaster. When the meat was done, I sliced it and let it marinate in cooking liquid for 48 hours. Because the refrigerator was full, I took the roaster outside and left it in a snowbank, hence the name. The roasts I made had an Italian flavor, but you can use any seasoning you like. The results will be pleasing no matter how you fix it. It isn't necessary to use an electric roaster, a Dutch oven or blue roaster will work just fine.

Preheat electric roaster of oven to 175 degrees
Season the roasts liberally with:
> **Italian seasoning**
> **Garlic salt**

Place the meat in the roaster and add:
> **Beef broth or game stock (about an inch on the bottom)**

Cook the roasts for six or seven hours. At the end of the cooking time, remove the meat and slice it as thin as possible, letting the slices soak in the broth or stock. Refrigerate or, if it's cold enough, put the roaster outside.

When it's time to serve, re-heat for an hour or two at 200 degrees. What could be simpler?

31

Venison Roast

Incredibly Easy Venison Pot Roast

When your guests eat this dish, don't tell them how easy it was to prepare.
Rather, let them think you spent all day slaving over a hot stove.

Preheat oven to 300 degrees
In a heavy-bottomed Dutch oven over medium-high heat, add:
> **2 tablespoons of olive oil**

When the oil is smoking-hot, brown until its crispy on all sides:
> **3 to 5-pound venison roast**

When the roast is completely browned, remove to a plate and deglaze the Dutch oven by pouring in:
> **1 cup red table wine**

Using a spatula, scrap up the caramelized bits from the bottom of the oven. When the wine has reduced to a few tablespoons, add:
> **A layer of onion slices**
> **Enough venison stock (or beef broth) to**
>   **cover ½ inch in the bottom of the oven**
> **The roast**
> **2 bay leaves**
> **rosemary and thyme to taste**
> **a layer of onions over the top of the roast**

Bring the stock to a boil, cover the Dutch oven and put in the oven for 3 to 4 hours, checking occasionally to be sure the oven isn't dry. If it is, add more stock.

When the meat is fork tender, remove to a warm plate and cover with tin foil. Remove the bay leaves, put the Dutch oven on a medium-hot burner and bring to a boil. When the stock boils, add just enough roux to thicken into gravy. Season with salt and pepper and serve over slices of the roast and potatoes.

This dish goes well with garlic mashed potatoes and a fresh green vegetable.

A Dutch oven with a tight-fitting lid is best for preparing this meal.
A dark venison stock imparts the best flavor, but beef broth or enhanced beef broth also works.
Browning the meat is a key. Searing all sides thoroughly seals in the juices. Use a tong rather than a fork to turn the meat. A fork will release too many of the meat's juices.

Venison Enchiladas

Venison Enchiladas

Preheat oven to 350 degrees

Soften flour tortillas in a frying pan with a few drops of oil. Fill tortillas with equal amounts of:

4 cups venison, cooked and shredded
4 ounces of diced chilies
1 can black olives, chopped
1 large tomato, chopped
½ medium onion, chopped

Roll up tortillas and place in a 9X12 glass baking dish. Bake for 1 hour, 15 minutes at 350 degrees.
Remove from oven and top with:

2 19-ounce cans of Enchilada red sauce
1 ½ cups cheddar cheese, shredded

Bake another 15 minutes.
Garnish with guacamole and/or sour cream.

Foiled Venison Chops

In a large square of tin foil, place:

2 venison chops, brushed with olive oil

Cover the chops with:

2 potatoes, thin sliced
1 green onion, thin sliced
½ red pepper
½ a zucchini, thin sliced
1 carrot, chopped

Season with:

Spike
Salt and pepper to taste

Seal the packet and place on a hot grill for 20 to 25 minutes, depending on the thickness.

Barbecue Meatballs

I like to use 1 pound of ground venison mixed with ½ a pound of ground pork.
If your venison is already mixed with pork, thaw 1 ½ to 2 pounds.

In a large mixing bowl, combine:

Meat   **¼ cup onion, chopped**
1 cup of fresh breadcrumbs **2 eggs**
fresh chopped parsley   **salt and pepper**
a little pinch of sage   **Brown the meat thoroughly in:**
                                4 tablespoons of butter

When the meatballs are browned, remove with a slotted spoon to a paper towel and let them drain. Next, place them in a covered sauté pan or crockpot along with 3 cups of your favorite barbecue sauce.

Allow the meatballs to sit until they've had a chance to soak up the sauce.

If you'd prefer to make your own barbecue sauce, combine in a sauté pan:

2 cups ketchup   **3 tablespoons Dijon mustard**
1 tablespoon liquid smoke   **3 tablespoons Worcestershire sauce**
¼ cup brown sugar   **4 tablespoons pineapple juice**
½ teaspoon paprika   **½ teaspoon chili powder**
1 tablespoon red wine vinegar **½ cup dry red wine**
salt and pepper to taste

Heat over medium heat, stirring constantly, until the sauce comes to a boil and is thoroughly mixed. Reduce heat and simmer for 10 minutes or more, stirring as necessary, until the sauce thickens.

Adjust the seasonings to taste. Add meatballs and let sit until the flavor of the sauce has been absorbed into the meat. Serve with crackers and cheese.

Venison Stroganoff

In a large skillet, combine:

2 pounds venison steak, cubed

2 tablespoons butter

1 medium onion, diced

8 ounces of sliced mushrooms

1 clove garlic, minced

When the meat is browned, set aside.

In another skillet, combine and bring to a boil:

2 cups milk

1 envelope onion soup mix

Thicken by adding small amounts of roux. Reduce heat and stir in:

Meat mixture

1 cup sour cream

Sautéed Venison Steak in Peppercorn Sauce

This recipe is very simple to prepare and it turns ordinary venison steaks into a delicious meal. One of the keys to this recipe is a reduced stock. You can accomplish this by simmering two cans of beef broth over very low heat until it reduces down to about a cup. The more it reduces, the more flavorful the broth becomes. It's even better if you make an enhanced broth.

Drain all the butter from the pan after removing steaks. Remember: Steaks will continue to cook when you take them out of the oven. Letting the steaks "rest" for a few minutes before serving allows the juices to reabsorb into the meat rather than running all over the plate.

Reducing the stock intensifies the flavor of the sauce.

Always use tongs rather than a fork to turn steaks. Puncturing steak with a fork will allow the juices to escape.

In a heavy-bottomed skillet over medium high heat, saute 4 venison steaks in:

1 tablespoon butter

You want to sear the steaks thoroughly on both sides, but do not finish the steaks in the pan. Place on a warm plate in put in a 190-degree oven before the steaks are finished. Allow the pan to cool for a few minutes, then add:

½ shallot, finely chopped

Over medium-high heat, pour in the skillet:

2 tablespoons Port
¼ cup Cognac

When most of the alcohol has burned off, reduce heat and add:

3 tablespoons reduced stock
4 tablespoons heavy cream
1 tablespoon green peppercorns

Remove steaks from the oven and allow them to rest a few minutes while you finish the sauce. Allow sauce to reduce and thicken slightly, then stir in:

2-3 tablespoons butter
salt and pepper to taste
few drops red-wine vinegar

Place steaks on warm plates and cover with sautéed mushrooms and peppercorn sauce.

Venison Stew

Here's a stick-to-your-ribs dish that easy to make and tastes great.

Preheat oven to 300 degrees
In a Dutch oven, heat:
>   **1 tablespoon olive oil**

In a Ziploc bag, combine:
>   **1 cup flour**   **1 tablespoon paprika**
>   **1 tablespoon salt**   **1 tablespoon fresh-ground pepper**

To the bag of seasoned flour, add and shake, coating thoroughly:
>   **1 pound venison cut into bite-size pieces**

Brown the meat thoroughly, adding:
>   **1 teaspoon dried thyme**   **1 large onion, quartered**
>   **2 large cloves garlic, minced**

When the meat has browned add, stirring with a wooden spoon to dislodge the
caramelized bits on the bottom of the Dutch oven:
>   **½ game stock (or beef broth)**

When all the bits have been dissolved in the stock, add and bring to a boil:
>   **3 ½ cups game stock (or beef broth)**

When the liquid boils, cover tightly and place in the oven for 2 hours. Remove and add:
>   **2 cups potatoes chopped in bite-size pieces**
>   **2 cups carrots chopped in bite-size pieces**

Return to the oven for another ½ hour. Near the end of that time, add:
>   **1 ½ cups sauteed mushrooms**
>   **1 cup frozen peas**

Cover and let sit until serving. The gravy should be thick at serving time. If it's not, mix
1 tablespoon corn starch in 1 cup white wine, stirring in a little at a time until the gravy thickens.
Season with salt and pepper and serve powder bisquits.

Stuffed Elk Peppers

Preheat oven to 350 degrees
Cut the tops off and remove the seeds from:

6 medium green bell peppers

Combine:

1 ½ pounds ground elk meat   **½ cup finely chopped onion**
1 cup cooked white rice   **¼ teaspoon seasoning salt**
salt and pepper   **1 clove minced garlic**

Pack the mixture into the peppers and place in a greased glass baking dish.
Combine and pour over the peppers:

½ cup water   **1 can of tomato soup**

Bake 45 minutes. Sprinkle with:

1 ½ cups shredded cheddar cheese

When the cheese is browned, remove from the oven and serve.

Breaded Caribou Chops

OK, so not everyone has a package of caribou chops in the freezer. This recipe works well with other big-game meats as well.

In a mixing bowl, combine:

1 cup of cracker crumbs

Dust the chops in flour, then dip in a mixture of:

2 eggs, beaten   **½ cup grated fresh Parmesan cheese**

Allow the excess to drip off, then coat with:

Cracker crumbs

In a large skillet over medium-high heat, combine:

Oil   **1 clove of chopped garlic**

Brown the chops quickly on both sides. Sprinkle with parsley flakes and allow to sit for a few minutes before serving.

Tarragon Venison Backstrap

This is another recipe that came to us from Randy Schoeck, our old friend from archery-maker Easton. Randy says this was a pleasant surprise that resulted from accidentally grabbing a bottle of tarragon leaves instead of basil flakes.

Wrap in bacon—using toothpicks to secure—and grill until the bacon is nearly burned off:

1 venison backstrap

While the meat is grilling, prepare sauce in a heavy skillet, starting by melting:

4 tablespoons of butter

When the butter is melted, add:

1 clove of garlic, minced

1 shallot, chopped

6 peppercorns

When the mixture begins to caramelize, add and reduce by half:

1 cup white wine or dry sherry

When the wine is reduced, add:

¾ cup crushed tarragon flakes

1 cup heavy cream

½ a cup of sliced mushrooms

salt and pepper to taste

Simmer the sauce to keep it warm. When the venison is done, slice it and smother the slices with sauce. Randy says this recipe is great with wild rice or new potatoes and a glass of Merlot.

Upland Game

Yogurt Gamebird with Cream Sauce

Yogurt Gamebird with Cream Sauce

In a mixing bowl, combine:

1 cup plain yogurt
¼ cup Dijon mustard
2 tablespoons fresh chopped dill (½ tablespoon dill weed)

In a skillet, melt:

2 tablespoons butter

Using a livestock syringe, inject ½ ounce of butter into each pheasant breast and refrigerate for at least an hour. When you're ready to prepare the dish, roll the gamebird fillets in the yogurt-Dijon mixture, coating thoroughly but not too thick, then roll them in:

1 cup cracker or cornflake crumbs

Place the breasts in a non-stick pan and bake at 350 degrees for 25 minutes or until done.
To make a simple sauce, combine in skillet:

¼ cup dry Vermouth
¼ cup pheasant stock (or chick broth)
2 tablespoons of butter

Boil down quickly, reducing to a syrupy consistency, then add:

1 cup heavy cream

Reduce the cream until the sauce begins to thicken, season with a squirt of lemon juice, salt and pepper and serve over the gamebird breasts, sprinkling with chopped parsley.

Outpost Lodge Pheasant

This recipe comes from Tom and Jill Olson, owners of the Outpost Lodge on the shore of Lake Oahe around Pierre, SD. We've enjoyed a number of trips to the Outpost Lodge, fishing for walleyes and hunting pheasants and waterfowl. Pierre is truly a sportsman's paradise. During one of our early trips, Jill whipped up this pheasant recipe and everyone raved about it. If you book a trip to Outpost Lodge, check out the menu for the spare ribs. Tom's barbecue sauce is out of this world. Unfortunately, I don't think he's going to share that recipe.

In a large mixing bowl, combine and soak for 2 hours:
> **4 pheasant breasts, skinned and halved**
> **2 cans of 7-UP**

Preheat oven to 350 degrees
In a large Ziploc bag, dust the breasts in a mixture of:
> **1 ½ cup flour**
> **Lawry's seasoning salt**
> **Pepper**

In a large skillet, brown the breasts in:
> **Cooking oil or butter**

Arrange the browned breasts in a baking dish and sprinkle with:
> **Garlic salt**
> **Chicken bouillon**

Cover with water and bake uncovered for 75 minutes
Toward the end of the baking time, combine:
> **2 cans cream of mushroom soup**
> **½ cup milk**

Drain off some of the water from the baking dish, add the cream-of-mushroom soup mixture and bake for one more hour, covered.

Pheasant Forever

We named this dish Pheasant Forever because it's a variation on a recipe we got from our friend Joe Duggan of Pheasants Forever, the Minnesota-based conservation organization. It can be prepared either in a 275-degree oven or a crock pot.

Skinless breast meat from 2 pheasants
1 cup flour
1 tablespoon parsley flakes
2 tablespoons chopped shallot
1/4 cup dry white wine
2 tablespoons flour

1 pint heavy cream
2 tablespoons olive oil
2 cups mushrooms, preferably morels
1 clove of minced garlic
2 tablespoons unsalted butter

Slice the breasts length-wise so you have four equal-sized pieces of meat. Sprinkle each piece liberally with lemon-pepper, cover and refrigerate for at least one hour. When you're ready to prepare, roll in flour and place in a cast iron skillet coated with olive oil over medium heat. Brown the breasts on both sides and remove to crock pot or a glass chafing dish (with a cover).

Next, add the mushrooms to the pan and sauté lightly until some of the juices are released. When they're in season and available, morels are the best choice, but portabellos, criminis, chantrelles or just about any mushroom or combination of mushrooms will work. Once the 'shrooms have released some of their juices, remove them to the crock pot or chafing dish.

Add the shallots and garlic to the pan for 30 seconds, then stir in the wine and allow the alcohol to evaporate. Add the cream and stir until all the flavors have combined. Strain the sauce through a fine sieve as you pour it over the meat and mushrooms. If you're using a crock pot, set it on low and cook for 3 hours (or more). If you use the chafing dish, place in 275-degree oven for 2 hours.

To thicken the sauce, prepare a roux by melting 2 tablespoons of unsalted butter and slowly stirring in 2 tablespoons of flour. Allow the roux to cool for 10 minutes, then stir it into the sauce for the final 15 minutes of cooking. Before serving, stir in parsley flakes and season with white pepper and salt.

Place one slice of meat and a spoonful of sauce over a bed of wild rice for each serving. Cornbread is a great go-along for Pheasant Forever.

Serves 4.

Pheasant Marsala

Gamebird Marsala

This very simple-to-make recipe is great, especially if you double the sauce and pour it over wild rice or wild rice-and-mushroom risotto. This recipe came from "Big Steve" Turiseva, travel coordinator for Babe Winkelman Productions. Sweet Marsala wine can be found with the cooking wines at most liquor stores. It's very inexpensive.

Preheat oven to 200 degrees

Slice in half length-wise, place between layers of wax paper and pound with a meat mallet:

Breast meat from 2 pheasants or ruffed grouse

Season the breasts with salt and pepper and roll in:

½ cup flour

Heat a heavy-bottomed skillet to very hot, then add:

3 tablespoons butter

Shake off the excess flour and brown the meat thoroughly in the butter, then place in oven on a plate.

Meanwhile, add to the skillet and brown well:

2 tablespoons of extra-virgin olive oil

1 cup sliced mushrooms

When the mushrooms are well browned and almost crispy, add and reduce by half:

1 cup sweet Marsala wine

When the wine has reduced, stir in:

½ cup heavy cream

small amount of roux to thicken the sauce slightly

Remove the meat from the oven and simmer in the sauce until the rest of the meal is ready. Just prior to serving, turn off the heat and stir in:

2 tablespoons of butter

salt and pepper to taste

1 tablespoon parsley flakes

If you double the sauce recipe you'll have plenty to pour over a bed of wild rice or wild-rice-and-mushroom risotto. It's a delicious combination.

Baked Pheasant with Asparagus and Blue Cheese

I love this recipe, and I don't just mean the meal. The actual recipe is great, as you'll see when you read it. It comes from Bob Musil, executive director of the Red Wing (Minnesota) Convention and Visitor's Bureau and was provided by Curt Johnson of the Minnesota Department of Tourism. I'm going to run it pretty much as written by Musil:

"Uncork a bottle of white wine and pour yourself a glass, taking care to reserve at least 1 cup for the recipe."

Fillet and bone the breasts from:

2 pheasants

In a mixing bowl, season with salt and pepper:

2 cups all-purpose flour

"Dust pheasant pieces in flour and brown in an oiled skillet. Arrange pieces in glass baking dish."

In a mixing bowl, combine:

1 can cream of chicken soup
1 ounce crumbled blue cheese
¼ cup white wine

Musil continues, "Pour mixture over browned pheasant pieces. Pour yourself another glass of wine, you deserve it. Bake in 350-degree oven for approximately 50 minutes or until sauce is bubbly and remaining wine is gone. Remove from oven and arrange 1 pound of asparagus spears on top. Cover with tin foil and bake an additional 15 minutes or until asparagus is tender when tested with a fork."

"Uncork another bottle of wine and serve dish with brown rice. Enjoy." Indeed.

Gamebird Tetrazinni

Here's a quick, easy recipe that can be thrown together in minutes and tastes great. It works with pheasant, ruffed grouse or any of the delicately flavored game birds.

Preheat oven to 350 degrees
In a large mixing bowl, combine:

2 cups gamebird, cut into small pieces   **7 ounces thin spaghetti, cooked**
1 can cream of mushroom soup   **1 can cream of chicken soup**
1 cup gamebird stock (or chicken broth)   **1 cup milk**
½ pound Velveeta, cubed   **5 drops tobasco sauce**

Place contains in a 9 X 13 glass baking dish. Top with:

Fresh grated parmesan cheese

Bake for 45 minutes.

Pheasant Cordon Bleu Casserole

Preheat oven to 350 degrees
In the bottom of a greased 9X13 baking dish, place:

4 to 6 pheasant breasts

Layer the breasts with:

5 slices of ham   **4 to 6 slices of Swiss cheese**
1 can cream of chicken soup   **½ can water**
2 cups stuffing mix

Pour over the top:

1 stick melted butter

Bake for 1 hour.

Pheasant Phingers

50

(There's Something Fishy About These)
Pheasant Phingers

While thumbing through a cookbook years ago we ran across a fish recipe that used Parmesan cheese and cracker crumbs.
We tried it, liked it and have been using it ever since. One night some guests suggested the same recipe might be good with pheasant
and we had to agree. We tried it using strips of breast meat and the results were impressive.
It works equally well with ruffed grouse and Hungarian partridge.

In a large mixing bowl, thoroughly mix:
> **6 eggs**

Dust in seasoned flour:
> **2 skinned pheasant breasts, cut in half length-wise to yield 4 thin pieces of meat**

Dip the breasts in the egg wash, then coat thoroughly with mixture of:
> **3 cups freshly-ground bread crumbs**
> **1 cup fresh grated Parmesan cheese**

In a large no-stick frying pan, melt:
> **½ cup clarified butter**

When the butter is hot, fry the meat until it's golden brown on each side.

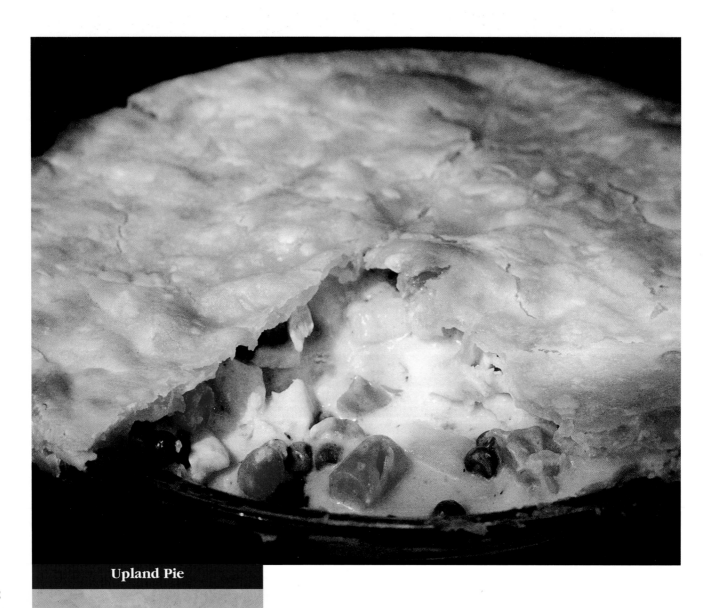

Upland Pie

Pheasant Dinner Pie

This recipe is a great way to utilize the meat left over from preparing a game stock.
It's relatively easy to make and provides a delicious meal that will easily feed four hungry people.

Preheat oven to 425 degrees
In the bottom of a 9-inch pie pan, roll out:
>**Half the pastry from a packaged pie crust**

In a small sauté pan over low heat, make a simple roux by combining and stirring until smooth and bubbly:

>**2 tablespoons butter**   **2 tablespoons of flour**

In a large skillet, bring to a boil:
>**1 ½ cups boiling gamebird stock (or chicken broth)**

When the stock comes to a boil, stir in the roux. Bring the roux-thickened stock to a boil for about a minute, then simmer, stirring occasionally for a few minutes (longer if possible).

Add and bring to a boil:
>**½ cup heavy cream**

Once the mixture comes to a boil, add the rest of the ingredients:

>**1 ½ cups bite-size pieces of meat from gamebird**   **¾ cup carrots, par-boiled**
>**¾ cup potatoes, par-boiled**   **½ cup frozen peas**
>**rosemary, thyme, salt and pepper to taste**

Pour into pie pan and cover with remaining pastry crust, trim and seal the edges. Cover the edge with 3-inch strips of tin foil to prevent excessive browning. Bake 35 to 40 minutes or until golden brown, removing foil for the last 15 minutes of baking.

You can get the meat necessary to make this meal by picking the bones of a pheasant or grouse carcass while you're making stock. Using tongs, remove the carcasses from the stockpot about an hour after the stock begins to simmer. That way the meat will still have plenty of flavor. The best meat can be found on the breastbone, around the wings, on the back and around the upper parts of the thighs. Pick what you need and return the carcass to the stockpot.

It's best if you allow the roux-thickened stock to simmer for half an hour, skimming any skin that forms on the surface. What you're making is what the French call a veloute` sauce, and it's delicious.

Seasoned Fried Quail

This recipe was provided by our friends at Quail Unlimited in South Carolina.

Split to, but not through, the breast bone:

8 quail

Combine in a large mixing bowl:

1 cup buttermilk
1 tablespoon hot sauce
2 tablespoons Worcestershire sauce
1 teaspoon dried thyme
salt and pepper

Mix thoroughly, add quail to the marinade and refrigerate for 8 hours. After 8 hours, remove quail, reserving marinade.

Dredge the quail in a mixture of:

1 cup all-purpose flour
½ teaspoon pepper
1 teaspoon red pepper
1 teaspoon paprika
1 teaspoon salt

Dip quail in the reserved marinade and dust in the flour mixture a second time. Then brown quail in a skillet with:

Vegetable oil

When the quail are golden brown (about 10 minutes) pour off all but 1/4 cup of the oil and add to the skillet:

½ cup chicken broth

Seasoned Fried Quail, cont.

Cover and cook over medium heat for 15 minutes. Transfer quail to serving platter, draining drippings and reserving ¼ cup in the skillet. Prepare a gravy by adding to the skillet and cooking over low heat, covered:

¼ cup all-purpose flour

Stir the gravy until it's smooth, gradually adding:

2 cups milk

Increase heat to medium, stirring constantly until the gravy thickens and begins to bubble. The final step is to stir in:

1 tablespoon Worcestershire sauce

salt and pepper

Serve the quail with the gravy

Quail over Rice

Preheat oven to 350 degrees

In a large mixing bowl, combine:

1 can cream of mushroom soup	**1 ½ cups cream**
1 can of mushrooms (reserving juice)	**3 cups of wild rice, cooked**
¼ teaspoon garlic salt	**¼ teaspoon celery salt**

Place in a glass baking dish, covering with the above mixture:

6 quail

Cook for 1 hour, covered with tin foil.

Combine in mixing bowl:

1 package onion soup mix	**mushroom juice**

Pour soup mix over the quail and cook, uncovered, another 15 minutes or until golden brown.

Pheasant Alfredo

Gamebird Alfredo

Pasta lovers will enjoy this recipe. I prefer to fix it with cheese-filled tortellini, which is available in the freezer section of most larger grocery stores, but any pasta will work. This recipe is excellent using the breast meat from any light-meat gamebird.

In a skillet, melt over medium high heat and combine:
> **4 tablespoons butter**
> **2 cloves garlic, diced**

Add and brown thoroughly on both sides:
> **2 skinned gamebird breasts**

Once the breasts are thoroughly browned, reduce heat to low, cover pan and allow to finish cooking.

Meanwhile, prepare in hot water:
> **1 pound tortellini, following instructions on package**

To another saucepan add 1 cup of water, place a collander or sieve over the top and steam until beginning to soften:
> **2 cups broccoli heads**

In another skillet, combine:
> **1 stick butter**

When the butter is melted, add:
> **1 cup heavy cream**

Quickly bring the cream to a boil, then stir in just enough roux to thicken the sauce slightly. Remove sauce mixture from heat, add the tortellini and:
> **1 cup freshly grated Parmesan cheese**
> **the broccoli**
> **bite-sized slices of the gamebird**
> **3 tablespoons pine nuts**
> **salt and pepper to taste**

Serve with garlic toast*

*To prepare a tasty garlic toast, cut a loaf of French bread into ½ inch slices. Melt one stick of butter and stir in garlic salt or garlic juice to taste. Dredge bread slices in butter, place on a cookie sheet and bake at 350 degrees until browned on each side. Toast can be prepared ahead of time

Pheasant Bundles

Pheasant Bundles

In a heavy-bottomed skillet over medium heat, melt 2 tablespoons of butter.
When the butter is hot and the foam subsides, stir in:

½ cup onion, finely diced   **1 large clove of garlic, finely diced**
1 cup mushrooms, diced   **1 cup of breast meat**

Simmer the ingredients until the meat is cooked, then deglaze the pan with:

¼ cup white wine

Season with:

Rosemary, salt and pepper to taste

When the wine is reduced, stir in:

½ cup heavy cream

Allow the cream to reduce to a few tablespoons, then puree the mixture in a blender or food processor. After the mixture is blended, add and puree for another few seconds:

1 teaspoon lemon juice   **1 tablespoon heavy cream**

Next, place a prepared piecrust on a cutting board, flatten slightly with a rolling pin and cut into 6 pie-shaped pieces. Brush each piece with melted butter. For a little extra flavor, gently blanche a dozen spinach leaves and place two leaves on each piece of dough. Spoon the bird mixture into the center of the dough and fold the corners to the middle. Seal the edges by pressing the dough with your thumbs, brush the outside with melted butter and place the bundles on a nonstick cookie sheet in a 400-degree oven for 12 to 15 minutes or until the bundles turn are golden brown.

To prepare the sauce, reheat the skillet and add:

½ cup dry sherry   **1 tablespoon of balsamic vinegar**
4 matchstick-sized slivers of fresh ginger

After the Sherry has reduced, add:

1 cup heavy cream

Simmer, stirring, until it's reduced by half and has thickened slightly. Strain the sauce and discard the ginger. Place a pheasant bundle in the center of a plate, drizzle a generous portion of sauce over the top and sprinkle with parsley.

Jeff's Fabulous Pheasant

This is a variation on a recipe we got from Jeff Garlie, owner and chef at The Landing, a little lake-side restaurant not far from where we live. Jeff and his wife Melissa worked for years in the Minneapolis-St. Paul area before deciding to open their own business in the lake country around Brainerd, MN. Jeff specializes in wild game, and this is one of the best meals on his menu. This recipe takes little time to prepare, but it's worth the effort, especially if you're entertaining.

Carefully trim the breast meat from 2 pheasants, using the carcass to make a stock. This can be done a day ahead of time. Or, if you have stock in your freezer, just place the carcasses in plastic bags and freeze them for another time.

To prepare the sauce:
In a heavy sauce pan, bring to a boil and reduce by half:
> **1 cup white wine**
> **2 cloves minced garlic**
> **1 bay leaf**
> **6 cracked peppercorns**

Add and simmer for 1 hour:
> **1 pint heavy cream**
> **2 cups stock (chicken broth will also work)**
> **Pinch of rosemary**

Thicken sauce with roux and simmer for 20 minutes, adding:
> **Salt and pepper**

Strain sauce.
In a saute pan, heat unsalted butter and add:
> **Sliced mushrooms (any variety will work)**
> **Chopped garlic**
> **1 tablespoon brandy**

When the mushrooms are browned, add to the sauce.

Fabulous Pheasant, con't

In a heavy-bottomed frying pan, melt 2 tablespoons of unsalted butter and add:
   Pheasant breasts, cut length-wise and rolled in seasoned flour
After the breasts have been browned, remove to a platter and inject with:
   Melted butter (optional. Use a livestock syringe, available at most veterinary stores)

Place browned meat in a casserole dish, pour on sauce, cover and place in a 200-degree oven for 2 hours.

Serve with wild rice or garlic mashed potatoes and a good Riesling or Chardonnay wine.

Mexican Wild Turkey

This is a great recipe for using up leftover turkey.
In a mixing bowl, combine:
   ¾ cup salsa
   1 can cream of mushroom soup
   1 soup can of milk
   ¼ cup onion, chopped
   ¾ cup melted butter
Tear into bite-size pieces:
   6 large flour tortillas
Combine in another bowl:
   1 cup grated cheddar cheese
   1 cup grated Monterey cheese
   Place ⅓ of the tortilla strips in a greased casserole dish and layer with ⅓ of the chopped turkey, ⅓ of the soup mixture and ⅓ of the cheese. Top with another layer of each and finish with the final layer, the cheese being on top. Cover and refrigerate overnight.
   Bake for 45 minutes in a 350-degree oven.

Peking Grouse

Peking Gamebird

This recipe is great with pheasant, ruffed grouse or any light-meat upland bird. It has some real zing!

Prepare skinned grouse or pheasant breasts on grill or by braising.
In a small bowl, combine:

> **4 tablespoons honey**
> **4 tablespoons soy sauce**
> **2 tablespoons minced fresh ginger**
> **2 teaspoons rice vinegar**
> **¼ teaspoon cayenne pepper**

Place meat in a glass baking dish, pour mixture over the top and bake at 325 degrees for 15 minutes or until glazed. Serve over a bed of white rice.

Upland Shorelunch

Upland 'Shorelunch'

Has this ever happened to you? You've reached the end of a long, successful day of upland hunting. The game has been cleaned, the gear is stowed and it's time to go home. But it's a gorgeous evening—there's a colorful sunset building on the horizon and off in the distance a wolf or coyote is breaking into song.

What's the rush?

Hunting is all about memories, and there's no better time to build memories than that last glorious hour of daylight. Why not drop the tailgate and enjoy the waning moments of the day with an upland "shorelunch"?

All it takes is a propane stove, a cast-iron skillet and a few simple ingredients. Start by cutting a bird or two into bite-size pieces and sprinkling them with Cajun seasoning. Fire up the stove and melt a stick of margarine.

When the margarine is smoking hot, toss in the meat and brown quickly on all sides.

Serve the bits with toothpicks and a dipping sauce, which can be made ahead of time. Simply combine equal parts Dijon mustard and honey, stir in some dill weed and you're good to go. If you prefer a hotter dipping sauce, add a little horseradish.

Kick back, pop a bottle of wine, nibble on your appetizers and relive those exciting moments spent in the company of good friends and spirited dogs.

Creamed Wild Turkey

Here's a great recipe for leftover turkey.

In a large skillet, thoroughly mix:

2 cups of milk	**1 teaspoon garlic sale**
2 tablespoons butter	**½ cup shredded cheddar cheese**
¼ cup chopped chives paprika	**salt and pepper**

Bring to a boil, then thicken by stirring in small amounts of roux. Reduce heat and add leftover turkey, simmering, covered for 10 minutes

Stuffed, Bacon-Wrapped Gamebird with Port-Mushroom Sauce

This delicious recipe works well with pheasant, ruffed grouse, quail, partridge or any light-meat upland game.

Preheat oven to 325 degrees
Start by preparing stuffing. In a small sauté pan, mix and heat until softened:

2 tablespoons butter
½ cup chopped shallot
½ cup chopped celery
1 clove chopped garlic

In a large mixing bowl, combine contents of sauté pan with:

2 cups prepared croutons (stuffing mix)
a pinch of sage
enough game stock (or chicken broth) to soften stuffing

Pour a tablespoon of extra-virgin olive oil in the bottom of large, cast-iron frying pan. In the bottom of the frying pan, lay:

3 slices of bacon per bundle

Stuffed, Bacon-Wrapped Gamebird with Port-Mushroom Sauce, con't

Place one breast over the bacon strips, cover with stuffing mix, top with the other breast, press firmly and wrap bacon completely around the bundle. Repeat with second bundle.

Place frying pan on burner and brown both sides of the bundles. When the bundles have browned, place frying pan in the oven, uncovered, for 30 to 45 minutes or until the bacon is crisp. Remove from oven, place bundles on a plate and allow to rest while you prepare the sauce.

To prepare sauce, first drain off all the bacon grease. Next, heat the frying pan over a medium-hot burner and add:

> **2 tablespoons of butter**
> **1 cup of chopped mushrooms**

When the mushrooms are well browned, pour into the pan:

> **½ cup Cognac**

Stir the Cognac, allowing the alcohol to burn off and the flavors to set in the mushrooms. Next, add:

> **½ cup Port**

Allow the alcohol in the port to burn off. When the liquid in the pan has become a thick syrup, pour in:

> **1 cup game stock (chicken broth will work)**

Stir until the mixture reduces and begins to thicken. Slice the gamebird bundles in half, pour the mushroom-port sauce over the top and serve immediately

Each bundle serves one person.

Braised Gamebird Supreme

This recipe takes its name from the delicious sauce served with it—sauce supreme.
The sauce isn't as difficult or time-consuming as it may appear and it's well worth the effort.

For the bird:
Preheat oven to 250 degrees
Slice length-wise, pound with a meat mallet and carefully pat dry:
Breasts of 2 pheasants or ruffed grouse (3 or 4 smaller birds)
Dust the meat in:
Seasoned flour
In a large skillet over medium-high heat, melt:
½ stick of butter
   Brown the meat thoroughly and quickly on both sides and place in a covered roaster or Dutch oven, adding:
2 cups of gamebird stock (chicken broth or enhanced chicken broth optional)
   Braise the meat for 90 minutes. Remove to a plate and place, covered, in the refrigerator until it's time for the final preparation.

To prepare the sauce:
In a saucepan over low heat, combine and stir until thoroughly blended:
3 tablespoons butter
3 tablespoons flour
In another saucepan, bring to a boil:
2 cups gamebird stock

   When the roux (flour and butter) is smooth and the stock has come to a boil, combine the two, stirring constantly. Bring to a boil for one minute, then reduce heat and simmer 30 minutes, stirring occasionally. What you are making is a "mother sauce" called sauce veloute`. Carefully skim any skin that accumulates on the surface during the 30 minutes.

Braised Gamebird Supreme, cont.

Next, stir in:

½ cup heavy cream
salt and pepper
a squirt of lemon juice

About 20 minutes before serving, combine the sauce and the gamebird from the refrigerator in a covered skillet and warm in a 250-degree oven until the rest of the meal is ready for the table.

Garlic mashed potatoes are a wonderful accompaniment for this dish. The flavors of the bird, the sauce and the garlic potatoes are a perfect blend. You can even scoop a little of the sauce over the potatoes. A green vegetable like string beans or fresh peas completes the entrée.

Serve with a chilled white wine like Chardonnay or Riesling.

Parmesan Pheasant

This delicious, easy-to-prepare recipe is a wonderful blend of flavors that's guaranteed to become one of the family's favorite dishes. This recipe works equally well for ruffed grouse, Hungarian partridge or any light-meat game birds.

To prepare the marinade, melt over low heat:

½ cup butter
1 tablespoon minced garlic
2 tablespoons Dijon mustard

Let simmer for a few minutes, stirring to blend, then remove from heat, allow to cool for a few minutes and blend in with a mixer until creamy:

1 egg white

In a deep-sided bowl, combine:

1 cup shredded Parmesan cheese
2 cups bread crumbs

Dip in the marinade:

Breasts of 2 pheasants, skinless, cut length-wise to yield 8 thin pieces of meat.

*Suggested wines:
A full-bodied Chardonnay or Riesling are excellent choices to accompany this meal.*

Roll the coated breasts in the bread crumbs, coating thoroughly. Remove each breast to a plate and sprinkle more bread crumbs over the top, packing the crumbs tightly against the meat. Cover the plate with plastic wrap and refrigerate for 2 to 24 hours.

When it's time to prepare the dish, heat in a non-stick skillet:

½ cup clarified butter

Brown thoroughly on both sides, flipping once. When the breasts are golden brown, remove to a large plate and place in a 350-degree oven for 10 minutes to finish cooking. While the meat is finishing in the oven, prepare:

Mustard butter sauce (page 139)

Remove the meat and place on individual plates, topped with sauce.
This meal is excellent with squash, pasta or rice pilaf.

Creamy Braised Upland Bird

This recipe takes a little time to prepare, but it's worth the effort. The end result is a melt-in-your-mouth dish drenched in a delicious cream sauce. This recipe will work with pheasant, ruffed grouse or any of the light-meat gamebirds. It also would be delicious with rabbit.

In a cast-iron skillet, place 2 tablespoons of olive oil and brown:

4 pheasant (grouse, partridge, quail) breasts rolled in seasoned flour

To prepare the sauce, combine in the same skillet used to brown the meat and reduce by half:

1 shallot, diced
2 bay leaves
6 black peppercorns
1 ½ cups of white wine (Sauvignon blanc is a good choice)

Add and simmer for one hour:

1 ½ pints of heavy cream
1 cup pheasant stock (chicken broth will work)
Rosemary or sage to taste

After an hour, thicken the sauce with roux, adding a little at a time until the desired thickness is obtained. While the sauce is simmering, place in a saute pan:

1 tablespoon chopped garlic
½ pound wild mushrooms
1 tablespoon butter

When the mushrooms are softened, add and bring to a quick boil:

⅛ cup brandy

Mix all the ingredients in a Dutch oven, season to taste with salt and pepper, add some sage or rosemary and place in a 250-degree oven for 2 hours.

Serve over a bed of wild rice or with garlic mashed potatoes and a glass of the same wine used in preparing the sauce.

When using gamebirds, I like to separate the breast meat from the tenderloins on the underside of the breast. The tenderloins are the tastiest part of the bird. Here's a little tip: After you brown the meat, place it in the refrigerator while you work on the sauce. Before putting the ingredients in the oven, inject the meat with a small amount of melted butter using a livestock syringe, available at most veterinary stores.

Deep-Fried Wild Turkey

Deep-Fried Wild Turkey

While the thought of deep-frying a turkey would probably give your grandmother a heart attack, it is truly a wonderful way to fix the bird. After eating a turkey (wild or domestic) fried in oil, you may never go back to the oven-baked version. The drawback to deep-frying a turkey is that it requires a lot of special, and somewhat expensive, equipment: a propane burner, a 30-quart stainless steel pot, a propane tank, lots of oil and a special thermometer. The good news is that once you try turkey (or a variety of other birds) in a deep-fryer, you'll use it so much it will more than pay for itself.

In the refrigerator, thaw a turkey (about 12 to 13 pounds is the maximum size)

Put enough vegetable or peanut oil in the pot to cover the bird (roughly 3 to 4 gallons) and heat to 350 degrees. One way to know for sure how much oil you'll need is to place the turkey in the pot and pour in enough water to cover. Remove the bird and mark the high-water mark on the inside of the pot. When filling with oil, put in just enough to reach that spot.

Inject the bird with a commercial butter-flavored marinade. Or, just use a pound of melted butter. To inject the bird, you can purchase a commercial injector or pick up a livestock syringe from a veterinarian or at a retailer who deals in farm and ranch supplies. When injecting the bird, make as few holes as possible. Insert the syringe into the breast and pump several ounces into one spot. Refill the syringe, put it into the same hole and inject several ounces into a different spot. Put three to five ounces in each breast and two to three ounces in each leg and thigh.

When the oil reaches 350 degrees, place the turkey in the basket and very slowly lower it into the pot. It's important to keep the temperature of the oil between 325 and 350 degrees.
The cooking time is approximately 3½ minutes per pound.

When done, the skin should be brown and crisp and the meat should be moist and flavorful. Allow the bird to rest 15 minutes before carving, allowing the juices to be absorbed into the meat.

Wild Turkey and Stuffing

Preheat oven to 325 degrees.

To make stuffing

In a large skillet, combine and sauté until soft:

½ stick butter

1 small onion, chopped

3 celery stalks, chopped

2 cups fresh mushrooms, sliced

1 clove of garlic, minced

In a large mixing bowl, combine ingredients from skillet with:

1 package croutons

1 cup wild rice, cooked

2 eggs

1 cup turkey stock (or chicken broth)

Slowly blend ingredients with a wooden spoon, adding stock until the mixture reaches the desired moisture. If you prefer a moist stuffing, add more stock. Season with:

Sage to taste

Rosemary to taste

Thyme to taste

Salt and pepper to taste

To make the turkey

Using a livestock syringe, inject the breast and thighs with:

½ stick melted butter

Thoroughly wash and salt the cavity of the bird. Spoon the stuffing into the cavity. Place in a roaster large enough to accommodate the turkey. To the bottom of the roaster, add:

1 inch of turkey stock (chicken broth)

Wild Turkey and Stuffing, con't.

Place in the oven, covered with tin foil. Baking time will depend on the size of the bird. It's done when the juices run clear. Remove tin foil near the end of the cooking time to brown the skin. When the bird is done, set aside, covered with tin foil.

To prepare the gravy:

Using a bulb baster, tilt the roaster and remove as much of the stock as you can without collecting any of the accumulated fat. Pour off the fat and place the roaster on a hot burner. Deglaze by pouring in:

½ cup dry white wine

Stir up all the caramelized bits, stirring with a wooden spoon. Pour the reserved stock in the pan, bring it to a boil and thicken with roux.

Season with:

Salt and pepper

Be careful not to overcook as turkey has a tendency to become dried out. When injecting the bird, make only one hole in each breast, moving the syringe around the breast without removing it. If you make too many holes, most of the butter will escape before it's cooked into the meat.

"Stuffed" Stuffing

This is a delicious way to prepare any light-meat game. It works equally well with pheasant, ruffed grouse, quail, Hungarian partridge, chukar partridge and even rabbit. It's fairly easy to make, requiring a minimum of prep time.

The idea behind this dish is to bake the meat inside a moist stuffing, which will add moisture and flavor to the meat We tried making this recipe without first braising the meat in game stock and it was good. But slow-cooking the meat in a good game stock prior to making the final dish definitely produces a moister, better-tasting dish. Not only does the meat taste better, but the reserved stock makes better wild rice and a more flavorful stuffing and gravy.

If you want to take a shortcut, eliminate the slow-cooking of the meat and simply place the browned meat in the stuffing mix and cook.

Start by breasting:

2 pheasants or ruffed grouse (3 or 4 birds if using smaller game like quail or partridge)

Season heavily with:

lemon-pepper

Pound the seasoning into the meat with a mallet. Roll the breast meat in seasoned flour (salt and pepper) and brown in a cast-iron frying pan with:

1 stick melted butter

Next, preheat the oven to 225 degrees. Set the frying pan aside to use later. Place the browned meat in a roasting pan and add:

2 cups game stock (canned chicken broth will work but homemade stock produces a better finished product)

Bake for two hours, tightly covered. Remove the meat from the roaster, reserving the liquids. Place the meat in refrigerator, covered, and let flavors set while you prepare the wild rice and stuffing.

In a saute pan, put 1½ cups of stock from roasting pan and 1 cup wild rice. Simmer until the rice is completely popped.

"Stuffed" Stuffing, con't

Set oven at 325 degrees.   In a small skillet, combine and fry until soft:
>**2 tablespoons butter**
>**½ cup chopped celery**
>**¼ cup chopped onion**
>**1 clove diced garlic**
>**1 cup mushrooms**

In a large mixing bowl, combine contents of pan with:
>**3 cups unseasoned stuffing mix or bread cut into small pieces**
>**1 cup of stock from roasting pan**
>**1 well beaten egg**
>**1 tablespoon dried sage**
>**¼ cup dried parsley flakes**
>**1 ½ cups of cooked wild rice**

It's important to make the stuffing mix quite moist. If it seems dry, add a bit more stock, another egg or a small amount of water. Mix with your hands until ready.

Place half the stuffing in a glass baking dish. Layer the game meat over the stuffing, then place the remaining stuffing over the top of the game. Place in heated oven, uncovered, for 30 to 45 minutes or until the stuffing is done.

Just before serving, heat the frying pan used to brown the meat. Pour in a little of the reserved stock from the roasting pan and use a spatula to scrap up the caramelized bits from the bottom of the pan. Stir in the remaining stock to make gravy. The gravy should thicken when the stock comes to a boil. If it doesn't, stir a tablespoon of cornstarch in a cup of white wine and add a little at a time until the gravy thickens. Season the gravy with salt and pepper and pour over the stuffing-game dish.

Fish

A Few Thoughts on Preparing Fish

As long as it's fresh or was properly frozen, making a great-tasting meal of fish is easy. Most of us have our favorite recipes and they almost always turn out great.

The most basic recipes involve dipping the fish in an egg wash, dusting the fillets in flour or cracker crumbs and pan-frying until their golden brown. Another favorite is deep-frying with a beer batter. We've included a number of such recipes in this cookbook.

But for those of you looking for different ideas we've also included recipes for dishes like fish cakes and poached fish, and have included lots of recipes for sauces that enhance the flavor of the meal. If you're looking for something different, check them out.

We're also including some tips for everything from cleaning, storing and freezing fish to breadings, cooking oils and flavor enhancements.

Getting the Fish Ready to Prepare

The first–and most important–job is making sure the fish fillets are thoroughly cleaned. If the fish is fresh, rinse each piece under a sprayer until it's completely washed and contains no slime. If the fish is frozen, remove it from the bag or container quickly, wash thoroughly and store in the refrigerator, preferably on ice. Never allow fresh or frozen fish to sit in water.

Here's a tip I got from an old-time guide/fish cleaner: Wash each fillet in a small amount of liquid dish soap. I know what you're thinking, but if the fillets are thoroughly rinsed before freezing or cooking, there will be no soapy taste. The soap washes away any remaining slime, which can spoil the flavor of the meat. That's especially true of northern pike.

Fish is best frozen in a vacuum-sealer that removes all the air and moisture from the bag. If you don't have a vacuum-sealer, use a Slide-Loc bag in water. Submerge the bag until only the partially-closed tab is exposed, using the water pressure to force air from the bag until it seals around the fillets. Remember, air and moisture are the enemies of frozen meat.

Cooking Oils

Fish can be fried in a variety of oils. Because it doesn't burn, clarified butter is one of my favorites. A 50-50 mix of butter and shortening is another good option. I also like canola oil and, on occasion, will use olive oil or olive oil mixed with butter.

Breading Options

The most basic coating option is seasoned flour. Start with two cups of flour and stir in small amounts of paprika, garlic salt, cayenne pepper, lemon pepper, onion powder, salt and white pepper. How much seasoning you use depends on your personal preferences. Even if I'm using breadcrumbs, beer batter or a commercial breading, I still like to "dust" the fillets in seasoned flour first.

Other breading options include cornmeal, cornflake crumbs, cracker crumbs and breadcrumbs. The easiest way to make crumbs is to place the cornflakes, saltines or fresh bread in a blender or food processor. Be sure to use fresh bread—the crust removed—and quality saltines. It does make a difference.

When using bread or cracker crumbs, I like to season the crumbs with a lot of Lawry's seasoning salt and garlic salt. For a more distinctive flavor, try some Cajun seasoning instead of Lawrys. Dust each fillet in seasoned flour, dip it in an egg wash, allow the excess to run off the fillet and finally roll it in the breading mix. Two well-beaten eggs mixed with a couple tablespoons of milk makes a good egg wash.

Skillets

After years of searching for a skillet that heats evenly, it's been my experience that a quality T-Fal pan is the best choice. An electric fry pan is another good option. I used to use cast-iron skillets, but they don't provide even heat.

The temperature of the oil should be around 350 degrees. Shake the pan frequently to make sure the fillets have an adequate amount of oil under them. Start with the skin-side down and turn the fillets only once.

If the fillets are done before the rest of the meal is ready, don't despair. Just place the fillets on a plate, sprinkle them with dill weed and pop in a 190-degree oven for a few minutes while you finish the rest of the meal. Don't leave them in the oven too long, however, or they'll get soggy.

Sauces

If a sauce is to be used with breaded fish, it's best to pour the sauce on the plate and lay the fillets on top of the sauce. That's because the breading will soak up sauce making it soggy. Laying the fillets on top keeps the fish crispy.

Cajun Catfish Tortellini

This recipe isn't just for catfish, it works well with walleye and a host of other fresh water fish as well.

Preheat oven to 190 degrees
Bring a large pot of water to a boil
In a mixing bowl, combine:

1 cup flour   **2 tablespoons of Cajun seasoning** (see below)

Sprinkle fillets of 2 fish (1 ½ to 2 pounds each) with:

Cajun seasoning

Dredge fillets in flour mixture and fry over medium heat in:

4 tablespoons butter

When the fillets are golden brown on both sides, place in the oven while you prepare the sauce and pasta.

In the boiling water, simmer until al dente:

12 ounces of cheese-filled tortellini

In the skillet used to fry the fish, combine and bring to a quick boil:

1 stick butter   **1 cup heavy cream**

Reduce heat and stir in:

Tortellini	**1 cup fresh-grated Parmesan cheese**
steamed broccoli	**pine nuts** (optional)

You can use a commercial Cajun seasoning, or make your own by combining:

1 tablespoon garlic powder	**1 tablespoon onion powder**
1 tablespoon fresh ground black pepper	**1 teaspoon cayenne pepper**
2 teaspoons dried thyme	**½ teaspoon oregano**

It's important to use the best tortellini you can find and to use a block of finely grated fresh Parmesan. Pre-grated Parmesan doesn't incorporate into the sauce as well as fresh-grated.

Fish Cakes

Fish Cakes

This recipe is great with just about any type of freshwater gamefish, especially when served with the lemon-butter sauce. It's a wonderful appetizer but also can be served as a main dish.

For the cakes:
Preheat oven to 190 degrees
In a glass baking dish, combine and put in oven:

1 pound of fresh fish fillets   **1 cup dry white wine**

When the fish is done—about 10 minutes—remove it from the oven and place in a large mixing bowl along with:

2 tablespoons of the poaching liquid   **½ cup shallots**
2 tablespoons green bell pepper   **2 tablespoons red bell pepper**
¾ cup fresh bread crumbs*   **1 tablespoon Dijon mustard**
1 tablespoon dried parsley   **1 teaspoon Worcestershire sauce**
2 tablespoons mayonnaise   **1 teaspoon Old Bay Seasoning**
1 tablespoon chopped bottled pimiento (optional)
a dash of lemon juice   **salt and pepper to taste**

When you grind the breadcrumbs, make a few extra. If the cakes are too wet, add enough breadcrumbs so they hold together

Blend the contents thoroughly with a wooden spoon. Now comes the hard part. Using a ½ cup measure, scoop up the contents, pressing tightly into the measure. Make patties by placing the mixture on a piece of wax paper and flattening slightly with a spatula.

In a food processor or blender, crush corn flakes until you have:

3 cups of ground corn flakes

Carefully lift the cakes from the wax paper with a spatula and coat them thoroughly in the corn flake crumbs. In a non-stick skillet, fry the fish in clarified butter until both sides are golden brown. Sprinkle with dried dill weed and place in the oven while you prepare the sauce. If you're not serving with a sauce, leave the cakes in the oven for at least 5 minutes to allow the flavors to set.

Serve with Lemon-butter sauce (page 137, 140, 141).

Northern Pike with Mustard-Dill Sauce

Pity the poor northern pike. It just doesn't get any respect. Once upon a time, for whatever reason, anglers across the pike's range
determined it was not fit for the table. Perhaps it's those annoying y-bones that many anglers don't know how to remove.
Perhaps it's the pike's disagreeable odor or the slime that covers its skin.
Or maybe it's those razor-sharp teeth that prompted anglers to treat pike like a second-class citizen.
Whatever the case, the pike is actually one of the tastiest of all game fish, as anyone who tries this recipe will understand.

Preheat oven to 190 degrees.

To prepare the fish

Wash fillets of pike, y-bones and lateral line removes. Pat dry and season with

Salt and pepper

Splash of lemon juice

In a large mixing bowl, combine:

2 eggs

1 cup of grated fresh Parmesan cheese

Dust fillets in flour, roll in egg wash and coat with:

Fresh breadcrumbs

Sauté pieces in clarified butter until they are golden brown on both sides. Places fillets in
warm oven while you prepare the sauce.

To prepare the sauce

In a small saucepan, bring to a boil:

2 cups chicken broth

While broth is coming to a boil, prepare a simple roux by combining in a small saute pan,
simmering and stirring until well blended:

2 tablespoons butter

2 tablespoons flour

Northern Pike with Mustard-Dill Sauce, con't.

Reduce heat and pour the roux slowly into the broth.
When thoroughly mixed, add, a little at a time:

¼ cup heavy cream
1 tablespon Dijon mustard
dill weed (fresh if available)

Taste the sauce as you go. You want the flavor to be quite strong. Add Dijon and dill weed accordingly. Finish the sauce with a splash of lemon, a tablespoon of butter and salt and pepper to taste.

Remove the fillets to a serving plate, douse with sauce and serve with garlic mashed potatoes and a green vegetable.

The sauce may taste a little strong, but it is the perfect accompaniment for the pike.

Fresh breadcrumbs and freshly grated Parmesan produce better results in most recipes. To make breadcrumbs, cut the crust off 8 slices of bread and process in blender or food processor until finely ground.

Parmesan Walleye and Alfredo

86

Parmesan Fish with Alfredo Sauce

This is an elegant dish that's sure to please the pasta lovers in any family.
It works equally well with walleye, crappie, perch, bass or just about any gamefish.

In a mixing bowl, combine:

1 cup fresh bread crumbs **½ cup fresh grated Parmesan cheese**
1 tablespoon fresh chopped parsley (optional)

In another bowl, mix:

1 large egg **2 tablespoons of milk**

Dip fish fillets in egg wash, shake off the excess and roll in bread crumbs, packing the crumbs into the fillets. Put the fillets in the refrigerator, covered with Saran Wrap, for one hour or more. Preheat oven to 190 degrees

To a large, non-stick skillet over medium heat, add:

1 stick clarified butter

Sauté the fillets until golden brown on both sides, then place in the oven while you prepare the pasta and Alfredo sauce.

In a large pot of water, simmer until done:

1 pound cheese-filled tortellini (or fettuccine)

In a large skillet, melt:

1 stick of butter

When the butter is melted, stir in:

1 cup heavy cream
1 cup fresh-grated Parmesan cheese
salt and pepper to taste

Drain the pasta, add to the sauce and shake the pan until combined. Top with:

Steamed broccoli
Pine nuts

Plate the pasta along with a couple pieces of fish. Serve with garlic toast and a good Chardonnay or Riesling wine.

Oven-Crispy Walleye

Preheat oven to 450 degrees
Thoroughly wash and pat dry:
> **6 walleye fillets**

Sprinkle fillets with:
> **Salt and pepper**
> **Garlic powder**

In a mixing bowl, combine:
> **¼ cup butter, softened**
> **¼ cup fresh parsley (chopped)**

In another bowl, beat:
> **1 egg**
> **¼ cup milk**

Spread the butter-parsley blend over the fillets, roll the fillets in the egg wash and dust with:
> **¾ cup fresh bread crumbs**
> **½ cup Parmesan cheese, finely grated**

Place fish in a buttered baking dish and bake until fish flakes and breading is golden brown

Spinach-Stuffed Fish Rolls

Preheat oven to 350 degrees
In a mixing bowl, combine:
> **8 ounces blanched, chopped spinach**
> **¼ cup grated Parmesan cheese**
> **4 tablespoons chopped onion**
> **¼ teaspoon tabasco sauce**

Spread mixture evenly across:
> **4 fish fillets**

Roll the fillets around the filling.
In a sauté pan, melt:
> **2 tablespoons butter**

Remove pan from heat and stir in:
> **1 small clove of garlic, minced**

Brush each roll with the butter-garlic mixture, place on a non-stick cookie sheet and sprinkle liberally with:
> **Paprika**

Place in oven until fish flakes. Serve with brown rice.

Sue's Fish and Chips

Sue's Fish and Chips

In pieces of aluminum foil, place:

8 fish fillets

Top fillets with:

Drops of lemon juice
8 tablespoons of butter
¼ cup onion, slivered
small canned shrimp
salt and pepper
juice of ½ lemon

Coat evenly with:

½ cup crushed potato chips

Carefully fold the aluminum foil and place on a hot grill until fish flakes

Grilled Walleye

This recipe was provided by Beth Jones, the wife of our friend Lloyd Jones, the former vice president for Delta Waterfowl.

Wash and place, skin-side down, on grill:
Walleye fillets, skin on. Baste with a mixture of:

4 tablespoons melted butter
½ teaspoon of paprika
½ teaspoon onion salt
¼ teaspoon black pepper

Continue to baste until fish flakes and skin
is blackened.

Fish Tacos

In a nonstick frying pan, heat:
> **¼ cup oil**

Season fish fillets with:

Salt and pepper	**Seasoning salt**

Dip fish fillets in egg wash, shake off excess and dust in:
> **Crushed cracker crumbs**

Fry until golden brown, then make tacos using the fish and:

Cheddar cheese	**Lettuce**
Salsa	**Sour cream**
2 cups shredded jack cheese	

Bake until cheese melts, top with sour cream and serve.

Hidden Valley Fish

This recipe was sent in by a reader of my syndicated newspaper column and it's pretty good.

Begin by combining in a mixing bowl:
> **1 cup sour cream**
> **1 cup mayonnaise**
> **1 package dry Hidden Valley Ranch dressing mix**

Coat the fish fillets with the sour cream-mayo mixture, then roll in:
> **1 cup cornflake crumbs**

Place the fish in a baking dish and put in a 350-degree oven for 30 minutes.

I experimented with an alternative to the ranch dressing mix with pleasing results. I substituted 1 tablespoon of lemon juice and dried dill weed. Either way, sprinkle some dried dill over the fish about five minutes before it's done. Fresh dill, if available, would yield even better results.

Mexican Walleye

Preheat oven to 350 degrees
In a nonstick skillet, heat:

¼ cup oil

Season walleye fillets with salt and pepper, then dust in:

1 cup seasoned flour

Fry fillets until golden brown, place in a shallow baking dish and cover with:

16 ounces green chili salsa

Top fish with:

2 cups shredded jack cheese

Bake until cheese melts, top with sour cream and serve.

Yogurt Crappies

Preheat oven to 375 degrees
In a mixing bowl, make an egg wash by combing:

2 eggs   **2 tablespoons milk**
1 teaspoon vegetable oil

Dip eggs in egg wash and roll in:

1 cup seasoned flour

In a nonstick skillet, melt:

¼ cup butter   **2 tablespoons vegetable oil**

Fry until brown on both sides. Remove to a shallow baking dish, and top with:

¼ cup yogurt   **1 ½ teaspoon dried dill weed**

Bake for 10 minutes, sprinkle with paprika and serve.

Easy Oven Crappies

Easy Oven Crappies

This is a quick, easy recipe for crappie or just about any other freshwater gamefish.

Start by preheating the oven to 500 degrees and washing the fish thoroughly, cutting into 2-inch squares and patting dry on paper towels. Next, combine in a mixing bowl:

¼ cup cornmeal
¼ cup fresh bread crumbs
¼ teaspoon paprika
½ teaspoon parsley flakes

In a small bowl, whip:

1 egg

You know the rest. Dip the fish in the egg wash, roll in the bread crumbs, shake off the excess and place on a cookie sheet in the oven until browned.

What could be easier?

Halibut Stuffed with Crab Meat

You say you went to Alaska and came home with several boxes of halibut? Maybe a neighbor or friend caught a big halibut and doesn't know what to do with it. One of the first trips Babe made to Alaska, he came home with this recipe and it quickly became one of our favorites. We don't always have halibut in the freezer, but when we do this is usually the recipe of choice.

Preheat the oven to 400 degrees.
In a frying pan, melt:

¼ cup butter

Saute until soft:

¼ cup chopped shallot

Next, stir in:

4 ounces of mushrooms   **1 can of crab meat**
½ cup of cracker crumbs   **2 tbls parsley**
Salt and white pepper to taste

Spread out in a large baking dish:

4 pieces of halibut

Cover the fish with the cracker-crumb mixture, then cover with:

4 more pieces of halibut

In a sauce pan, melt:

3 tablespoons butter

Blend and stir until thickened:

3 tablespoons flour   **Salt**
1 ½ cups milk   **½ cup white wine**

Pour the sauce over the fish and bake for 25 minutes. Remove from oven and sprinkle with:

1 cup of shredded Swiss cheese

Return to oven for 10 additional minutes and serve. Serves 6.

Fish in Wine Sauce

We've run across half a dozen versions of this recipe. While this is our own adaptation, it is fairly true to the original French recipe. It was intended for sole or flounder, but it works very well with walleye and would be good with any dry, delicately flavored white fish. It works best with larger fish (three- to four-pounders).

To prepare, layer the washed, boneless, skinned fillets in a buttered, ovenproof glass baking dish, season with salt and pepper and top with:

2 tablespoons of shallots, finely chopped
2 tablespoons of butter chopped in small pieces
1 ½ cups cold fish stock or "emergency" fish stock
2 cups mushrooms, chopped and sautéed in butter

Cover the baking dish with parchment paper and simmer for a few minutes on the stovetop, then place in a 350-degree oven for 10-12 minutes or until the fish flakes. When the fish is done, pour the poaching liquid into a saucepan and reduce to 1 cup over high heat. While the poaching liquid is reducing, make a paste by stirring together:

2 ½ tablespoons flour
3 tablespoons soft butter

When the liquid has reduced, turn off the heat and stir in:

the flour-butter paste
½ cup heavy cream

Return the sauce to a boil, adding more cream as necessary if the sauce becomes too thick. Season with salt and pepper and a splash of lemon juice. Pour the sauce over the fillets and top with:

⅓ cup Swish cheese, shredded
1 tablespoon of butter pieces

Place under the oven's broiler for several minutes until the cheese is melted and beginning to brown. Remove dish from oven and sprinkle with:

1 tablespoon of fresh chopped dill
(or a smaller amount of dried dill)

Serve with a Chardonnay or Riesling.

This is an elegant dish that could easily be overpowered. For that reason it's best served with rice or boiled potatoes. When using a walleye or any fish 3 pounds or larger, it's a good idea to remove the lateral line (the dark meat down the center of the fillet).

Parmasan Walleye

Parmesan Walleye

Fine restaurants offer the ultimate dining experience. Whenever I encounter a special meal, I try to analyze every aspect of the dish, from the spices and herbs used to make the sauce to the way different flavors complement one another. Then I go home and try to recreate the meal in my own kitchen.

While I'm usually not able to duplicate what the chef prepared, I often find the results are pleasing in their own right. A good example is "champagne shrimp", a popular dish at The Landing, a local restaurant owned by Jeff and Melissa Garlie.

I love the taste of the champagne sauce, especially when poured over wild rice, so I tried to duplicate it. What I came up with wasn't the same as Jeff's, but was so good I worked up this recipe for "Parmesan fish with champagne sauce". I made it with walleye, but about any of the light game fish will work.

To prepare the fish, season with salt:
> **2 fillets (the size of a 2-pound walleye)**

In a mixing bowl, thoroughly combine:
> **3 eggs**
> **½ cup Parmesan cheese, freshly grated**

Dust the fillets in flour, dip in the egg/Parmesan mix and roll in:
> **Fresh bread crumbs**

In a non-stick skillet, brown the fillets on both sides over medium heat in clarified butter. While the fillets are cooking, prepare the sauce. In a sauce pan over medium heat, combine:
> **2 tablespoons shallots, finely chopped**
> **½ cup champagne (Asti)**
> **1 teaspoon dried basil**

When all but a few tablespoons of the champagne have boiled away, stir in 1 cup of heavy cream or crème fraiche. Simmer for a few minutes, adding some fresh chopped basil leaves if available. Finish with salt and pepper.

Fish Appetizer

In a sauté pan, combine:

1 stick butter

1 small bunch green onions, chopped

Add:

1 tablespoons flour

½ pound grated Swiss cheese

1 pint half and half

When cheese has melted, add:

1 tablespoon Sherry

salt and pepper

1 pound cooked, flaked fish

parsley

Serve with Melba toast or crackers

Walleye-Wild Rice Cakes

My friends know I never miss the opportunity to use wild rice in a recipe. One day I was experimenting with a new recipe for walleye cakes and decided to use some leftover wild rice in making the cakes. The results were so pleasing I added it to my recipe file.

Preheat oven to 400 degrees
In a small glass baking dish, combine and bake until the meat is flaky:

Fillets from one walleye (about 4 oz. each)
½ cup white wine

Remove from oven and crumble the meat into a large mixing bowl along with:

½ cup wild rice, cooked
¼ cup onion, finely diced
2 tablespoons green bell pepper, finely diced
2 tablespoons red bell pepper, finely diced
½ cup fresh bread crumbs
1 tablespoons Dijon mustard
2 tablespoons mayonnaise
2 eggs, beaten
a squirt of lemon juice
1 tablespoon Worcestershire sauce
salt and pepper

Using a half-cup measure tightly packed, scoop the contents onto a piece of wax paper and flatten with a spatula. Sprinkle the top with:

Fresh ground bread crumbs

Using a spatula, turn the cakes and carefully cover the other side with bread crumbs until both sides are thoroughly coated.

Cover the cakes with another sheet of wax paper and refrigerate for several hours. Refrigerating will help keep the cakes from crumbling.

When it's time to prepare the cakes, fry them in a large non-stick skillet until golden brown on both sides using:

½ cup clarified butter

Cracker Crumb Fish

Cracker-Crumb Fish

Start by crushing in a food processor or blender:

1 bag premium saltines

Be sure the crumbs are ground to a fine powder. If you don't have a food processor or blender, place the saltines in a Ziploc bag and crush them with a rolling pin. Season liberally with:

Garlic salt

Lawry's seasoning

Lemon-pepper

In a separate bowl, mix:

2 eggs

¼ cup milk

Place washed fillets on a paper towel and pat them dry. Dust fillets in flour, shake off the excess, dip in the egg wash and roll in the cracker crumbs until thoroughly coated.

In a large, non-stick frying pan, melt over medium-low heat:

Equal amounts of butter and butter-flavored shortening

Optional: Canola oil

When oil begins to sizzle, place fillets in the pan and fry until brown on both sides.

Preheat oven to 190 degrees. When fillets are done, place fillets on an oven-proof plate and season liberally with dill weed. Place in oven for 10 minutes while the rest of the meal is finished.

Placing the fillets in the oven allows the flavors to set.

Salt and pepper to taste and drizzle with fresh lemon juice.

Fish Cakes

A great appetizer can be the highlight of any meal, and this is one of my favorites. I like to use half a pound of fresh fish along with half a pound of crab meat. Fresh crab meat is best, but canned also works.

Place in a strainer over a saucepan of boiling water until flaky:

½ pound fresh fish

Combine steamed fish with:

½ pound crab meat

In a skillet over medium heat, pour:

2 tablespoons of olive oil

When the oil is hot, add and cook until softened:

1 tablespoon diced red bell pepper   **1 shallot**

1 teaspoon minced garlic   **1 finely diced mushroom**

In a large mixing bowl, combine the fish and vegetables with:

2 egg whites, whipped to a froth   **1 tablespoon Dijon mustard**

¼ cup fresh parsley   **Salt and pepper**

4 tablespoons finely crushed cracker crumbs

Under a broiler oven, slightly brown 2 cups of fresh breadcrumbs, moistened slightly with olive oil. Shape the fish mixture into tight balls the size of golf balls, then flatten into patties. Press the patties into the breadcrumbs, coating thoroughly and placing each on a layer of waxed paper. Refrigerate the patties for at least two hours, allowing them to set. The patties can remain in the refrigerator overnight.

Using a spatula, place the patties in a non-stick skillet over medium heat in:

¼ cup clarified butter

Brown thoroughly on both sides, turning once. The cakes may be a bit crumbly, so be sure to turn them gently using a spatula.

Place the finished cakes in a 190-degree oven and serve them with lemon-butter sauce (page 137).

Crispy Stuffed Fish

This recipe goes great with just about any of the bigger freshwater game fish. We've enjoyed it with walleye and northern pike and suspect it would go well with bass and even catfish.

Preheat oven to 300 degrees.

To prepare the stuffing:
Melt in a sauté pan over medium heat:
    3 tablespoons butter
Add, cooking until soft:
    ¼ cup finely chopped onions   **¼ cup finely chopped celery**
    1 clove garlic, minced
Remove from heat and pour into a mixing bowl with:
    1 cup fresh breadcrumbs   **2 tablespoons finely chopped fresh parsley**
    Enough game stock to moisten crumbs
Mix by hand, adding for seasoning:
    A dash of lemon juice   **Salt and black pepper to taste**

To prepare the fish:
    Cut fillets of larger fish in half length-wise. Arrange fillets in a glass baking dish, buttered to coat the bottom. Salt and pepper each side and dribble a little lemon juice over the fillet. Pile stuffing mix on top of fillet, pressing firmly. Place the other half of the fillet over the top.

    To prepare the crispy topping:
Crush with your hands and mix with melted butter:
    1 cup corn flakes
    When the corn flakes are wet enough to stick, layer them over the top of the fillets to form a heavy crust. Place baking dish in the oven and cook until the fish is done.
    Serve with Mushroom-cream sauce (page 147)

Delta Baked Fish

This recipe came from Beth Jones, wife of former Delta Waterfowl Foundation Vice President Lloyd Jones. Delta is one of our favorite conservation organizations and this recipe is one of our favorite ways to prepare walleye or just about any light-meat gamefish.

In a glass baking dish (10 X 15) place fish pieces, seasoned with salt and pepper. Coat the pieces with a mixture of:

2 tablespoons melted butter
1 tablespoon fresh lemon juice
1 tablespoon Dijon mustard
1 tablespoon parsley flakes

Bake in a 350-degree oven until the fish begins to turn white (about 8 minutes)
In a dish, mix:

1 tablespoon melted butter
1 ½ cup crushed Rice Chex or cornflakes.

Coat the fillets thoroughly with the mix and return to the oven until the fish slakes and the topping is golden brown.

Top fillets with lemon-butter sauce.

It's in the Bag

Preheat oven to 400 degrees
In a large Ziploc bag, combine and shake until mixed:
> **½ cup cornmeal**
> **½ cup flour**
> **1 teaspoon lemon-pepper**
> **salt and pepper**
> **½ teaspoon garlic salt**

Add fish fillets to bake and shake until coated. Place fillets in a glass baking dish and brush with:
> **½ stick melted butter**

Coat the fillets with:
> **1 cup sliced almonds**

Place in oven until golden brown.

Mushroom-Baked Fish

Preheat oven to 350 degrees
In a medium skillet, melt:
> **8 tablespoons of butter**

Stir in:
> **1 tablespoon of lemon juice**
> **salt and pepper**

Roll fish fillets in the mixture, then place in a shallow baking dish. Top the fillets with:
> **⅓ cup mushrooms, sliced**
> **2 tablespoons onion, finely chopped**

Spoon remaining butter over the fillets and bake 15 to 20 minutes, until fish flakes.

Baked Crappie Divine

Preheat oven to 400 degrees
Coat the bottom of an oven-proof pan with butter and layer with:
6 crappie fillets
Over the top of the fillets, pour:
1 stick melted butter
fresh chopped parsley
Cajun seasoning (to taste)
Bake until the fish is flaky, the sprinkle liberally with:
Lemon juice

Baked Fish with Honey-Lemon Sauce

Preheat oven to 450 degrees
In a glass baking dish, place fillets of fish and coat with:
2 tablespoons of honey
salt and pepper to taste
¼ cup onion
In a small saucepan over low heat, combine:
½ stick butter
¼ cup Vermouth
4 tablespoons lemon juice
Simmer butter – vermouth mixture several minutes, then pour over fish.
   Place in oven and bake, uncovered, for 20 minutes. After 20 minutes, reduce heat to 300, cover with aluminum foil and bake another 15 minutes.

Fish Delight

Preheat oven to 350 degrees
In a mixing bowl, combine:

1 cup cream cheese
1 cup Miracle Whip
pepper
garlic salt to taste

Spread the mixture over:

4 fish fillets

Place fillets in a greased baking dish and sprinkle with:

Chopped onion

Bake covered until fish flakes. Cover fillets with:

1 ½ cups shredded Swiss cheese

Cajun Walleye

In a medium mixing bowl, combine:

½ cup cornmeal
½ cup flour

Season both sides of fish fillets with:

Cajun seasoning

Dust fish in cornmeal mix, then fry until golden brown in:

2 tablespoons Canola oil
2 tablespoons butter

Thai Fish

Preheatoven to 400 degrees

Season 4 fish fillets with:
Lemon pepper
Fresh dill, chopped
Salt

Lay fillets in a glass baking dish and place in oven until fish flakes. In a mixing bowl, combine and cover the fish with:
⅔ cup buttermilk
5 tablespoons mayonnaise
1 tablespoon Thai seasoning
chopped dill

Return to oven long enough to heat the sauce. Serve immediately

A Few Thoughts About Wine

Partaking of the wild harvest is the final and ultimate celebration of the outdoor experience. Whether meal the gracing your table is wild turkey or walleye, nothing complements the flavor of wild cuisine and turns the meal into a special occasion like a glass of good wine.

But unless you happen to be a student of wine, finding an affordable bottle of table-ready wine can be as big a challenge as bagging a trophy whitetail. It doesn't have to be that way.

Today's shopper has at his/her disposal a wide variety of affordable wines that are ready to be uncorked and enjoyed. Thanks to the proliferation of wineries in California, Washington, Oregon, Australia and elsewhere, quality wines are now quite inexpensive. In fact, it's possible to buy an excellent bottle for $10 or less.

If browsing rack after rack of wines leaves you a bit light-headed, here are some tips for picking the right bottle for your next special event.

Tip No. 1. When you visit your favorite liquor store, ask to speak to someone who's an authority on wine. Tell that person what's on the menu, specify a price range and be sure to request a bottle that is properly aged and ready to drink. Most spirits shops have several people who can steer you in the right direction, some even allow you to sample recent releases.

Tip No. 2. When eating in a restaurant with a good wine list, ask the waiter or wine steward for suggestions. If you like the wine delivered to your table, make a note not only of the grape and the winery, but also the vintage. Just because a particular vineyard's 1997 Chardonnay was superb doesn't mean its 1999 will be as good.

Tip No. 3. Subscribe to or pick up a copy of a magazine like Wine Spectator. In the back of each month's Wine Spectator you'll find a long list of new releases, including a section on "best buys" along with the suggested retail price. Best of all, the magazine notes if wines are ready to "drink now" and how long they can be stored in a cellar. Wines that are served "before their time" can be very acidic. Again, note not only the name, but the vintage as well.

Duck Delights

Duck Delights

Preheat oven to 250 degrees
In a large skillet, brown in butter:

> **Breast of 1 duck**

Place breasts in a covered roaster and add:

> **1 ½ cups homemade duck stock (or ¾ cup beef and ½ cup chicken broths)**
> **2 bay leaves**   **½ teaspoon rosemary**
> **½ teaspoon thyme**

Braise ducks for 2 hours. When the duck is cooked, remove it to a plate and increase oven temperature to 350 degrees. If you wish to make a gravy, reserve the braising liquid.

In a large mixing bowl, combine:

1 teaspoon of minced garlic	**1 can cream of mushroom soup**
8 ounces softened cream cheese	**¼ cup chopped carrots**
1 cup of duck meat, chopped or shredded	
⅛ cup heavy cream	**½ of a small onion, chopped**
salt and pepper	

On a smooth work surface, spread out the triangles of readymade crescent rolls and spoon the duck mixture over the dough. Fill the triangles until you run our of mixture. Close the rolls, brush the surface with melted butter and pat each in crushed croutons or fresh breadcrumbs.

Place on an ungreased cookie sheet and bake until golden brown, about 25 minutes. Serve with potatoes or wild rice.

To prepare gravy:
Strain the braising liquid, removing the bay leaf, and bring to a boil. Stir in a small amount of roux or corn-starch mixed in cold water or white wine. Stir until it reaches the desired consistency and pour over potatoes or rice. You can even pour some over the "duck delights."

Braised Canada Goose with Orange Sauce

114

Braised Canada Goose with Orange Sauce

Too many of the recipes for Canada goose I've tried produce a dry, flavorless product. That's a shame, because Canada goose is a wonderful-tasting bird if you know how to fix it. Here's a recipe everyone in your family is sure to enjoy. Because Canada geese vary greatly in size, you may have to make some adjustments if you're fixing a bird that weighs 10 pound or more. This recipe is for an average-sized (5 to 7 pounds) bird.

Preheat oven to 250 degrees

Thoroughly wash, inside and out, the cavity of the goose or geese to be prepared.

Stuff each cavity with:

½ onion   **3 carrot sticks, chopped**
3 celery stalks, chopped

Place the bird in a roasting pan and add:

2 cups homemade goose stock (or enhanced chicken broth)
1 cup red wine

Place in oven, covered, for 2 hours or until the juices run clear. Remove the cover for the final 15 minutes or until the skin is brown and crispy. De-bone the bird, keeping the breast and leg/thigh in one large piece. Set aside, covered.

Remove the fat from the roasting pan using a bulb baster or large spoon. Strain the braising liquid carefully through cheesecloth, then place in a saucepan over medium-high heat, stirring in:

¾ cup fresh orange juice   **½ cup dry red wine**
¼ teaspoon dry mustard   **salt and pepper**

To thicken the sauce, add a little roux or cornstarch dissolved in white wine or cold water. Taste and adjust the seasonings. When you've achieved the desired flavor, add the goose pieces just long enough to warm. Serve with wild rice or mashed potatoes.

Gourmet Duck

Think duck is always dry and tough? This quick, easy recipe is a fool-proof way to make moist, flavorful duck.

In a large skillet, combine and saute until tender:
> **¼ cup butter**
> **2 celery stalks, chopped**
> **1 ½ cup mushrooms, chopped**
> **½ cup carrots, chopped**

In a large frying pan, melt:
> **¼ cup butter**

To the butter, add:
> **1 jar current jelly**

When the jelly melts, stir in and bring to a boil:
> **1 ½ cup bourbon**
> **1 ounce dry sherry**
> **salt and pepper**

When the mixture comes to a boil, add:
> **2 duck breasts**

Boil for 15 minutes, then turn and boil for another 10 minutes.

Roast Goose

Here's a way to "cook your goose" so it comes out tender and tasty.

Preheat oven to 300 degrees

In a Dutch oven over medium heat, fry up:

3 pieces of bacon

When the bacon is crispy, set it aside on a plate and make yourself a BLT. But first, use the grease to thoroughly brown the skinless breasts of:

1 large goose, seasoned with salt and pepper

Make sure you brown the meat completely, sealing in the juices.

When the meat is browned, add to the Dutch oven:

1 ½ cups of game stock (preferably made from a goose carcass)
1 cup white wine
2 medium onions, peeled and sliced
thyme
3 bay leaves

Bring the braising liquid to a boil, then place in the oven for 4 hours, covered, replacing any liquid that boils away in the process.

When the meat is tender, remove and set aside on a warm platter. Pour the braising liquid through a sieve and discard the vegetables. Return the liquid to the Dutch oven on a medium-hot burner, bring the liquid to a boil and add a tablespoon of cornstarch thoroughly dissolved in a glass of wine. Stir until the liquid thickens into a gravy. Slice the meat and pour the gravy over meat and a side dish of potatoes or wild rice.

Starters & Side Dishes

Oriental Grouse Salad

Oriental Grouse Salad

This is Babe's favorite recipe. It's one of mine, too.

In a large bowl, place:

1 head of Napa lettuce in bite-size pieces

Toss with:

8 ounces of fresh mushrooms, sliced

1 cup slivered almonds

1 can of water chestnuts, drained and sliced

In another bowl, combine:

1 cup mayonnaise

¼ cup soy sauce

Top the lettuce with:

2 cups grilled ruffed grouse breast

the mayonnaise-soy sauce

1 cup chow mein noodles

Venison-Wild Rice Soup

This is a great recipe that incorporates delicious wild rice with the rich flavor of ground venison. The venison is best if spiced with some sausage seasoning. It's easy to make and is a real crowd-pleaser.

In a large skillet, brown and drain:

1 pound ground venison, seasoned.

To the skillet, add, cooking until it bubbles:

1 cup whole milk
2 cans cream of potato soup
2 cups cooked wild rice

Add:

1 carrot, grated

Simmer for a few minutes, season with salt and pepper and (if desired) a small amount of sage and serve.

Venison Rumaki

This is a great, easy-to-make appetizer.
Cut into chunks the size of a water chestnut:

Venison steak

Marinate meat at least 1 hour (preferably overnight) in:

Teriyaki sauce

Place a chunk of meat on each side of a water chestnut. Wrap in bacon, securing with a toothpick. Place on a lightly greased cookie sheet and bake in a 400-degree oven until the bacon is crisp.

Gamebird/Wild Rice Soup

This great-tasting, easy-to-prepare dish is a wonderful starter, but also hearty enough to serve as a complete meal. The secret is in slow-cooking the game in a good homemade broth to add flavor and tenderness. If you don't have a game stock, prepared chicken broth also works. One of the next things about this recipe is that it can be made utilizing bits and pieces of meat that might otherwise go to waste. If you breast your game birds (pheasant, ruffed grouse, quail, partridge or whatever) you'll notice little bits a pieces of meat on the carcass that are left behind. These include the meat around the wings and under the wishbone, the back meat and slivers of meat along the breastbone. Trim these pieces of meat and save them in a Ziploc freezer bag, adding to the bag until you have about a pound of meat. Or, just take a couple of breasts and cut them into bite-sized pieces to prepare this dish.

Preheat oven to 225 degrees

Start by seasoning the chunks of meat liberally with lemon-pepper or an all-purpose seasoning like Spike. In a Ziploc bag, season:

1 cup all-purpose flour with salt and pepper

Toss the meat chunks in the flour until coated, then brown in a cast-iron frying pan with:

½ stick butter

When the meat is thoroughly browned, set aside the frying pan and place the meat in a roaster pan and cover with:

2 ½ cups game stock (chicken broth)

Place in oven for 2 hours.

When meat is thoroughly cooked, remove the roaster from the oven, reserving the stock. Cover the meat and place in the refrigerator.

In a covered saucepan, combine and cook until it pops:

1 cup uncooked wild rice   1 ½ cups reserved stock from roasting pan

Deglaze the frying pan by adding ½ cup of the stock, scraping up the caramelized bits with a spatula. Stir in another ½ cup of stock along with:

1 cup of half and half   2 cans cream of potato soup
2 cups of cooked wild rice   1 carrot grated
cooked meat

Simmer until warm. Serve with crackers or powder biscuits.

You can spice this dish up by adding sautéed onions or even a few sautéed mushrooms.

Crunchy Mashed Sweet Potatoes

This unique dish takes a bit longer to prepare than most of the sweet potato or squash recipes, but it's worth the effort.

Preheat oven to 350 degrees.

Peel, cut into small pieces and boil until done in salted water:

5 large sweet potatoes

When they're tender, drain and mash the sweet potatoes.

In a large mixing bowl, beat together:

3 large eggs

2 tablespoons of maple syrup

2 tablespoons of vanilla extract

Add the mashed sweet potatoes and blend thoroughly. Transfer to a buttered glass baking dish.

For the topping, blend:

¾ cup brown sugar

4 tablespoons of chilled butter

Sprinkle the brown sugar over the potato mixture, then top with:

1 ½ cups of crushed corn flakes

Bake for 1 hour, let sit for 10 minutes and serve.

Mashed Potatoes and Sweet Potatoes

Few side dishes I've served got the ooohs and aaahs this one did. It goes great with barbecue dishes.

Preheat oven to 350 degrees
In a small piece of tin foil, combine and place in the oven:
> **6 large cloves of garlic, peeled and cut in half**
> **a few drops of olive oil**

Bake the garlic until soft, about 20 minutes
In a large covered pot, combine:
> **2 pounds potatoes, peeled and cut into chunks**
> **2 pounds sweet potatoes, peeled and cut into chunks**
> **½ teaspoon dried rosemary**

When the potatoes are done, drain the water and mash with:
> **Heavy cream (just enough to achieve desired consistency)**
> **roasted garlic**
> **4 tablespoons of butter**
> **salt and pepper**

Spoon the mashed potatoes into a glass baking dish, cover and allow to sit at room temperature for an hour or two. Allowing the dish to rest allows the flavors to infuse. Finish by placing in a 350-degree oven for 30 minutes or until the top begins to brown.

Garlic-Herb Mashed Potatoes

Over the years I've seen dozens of recipes of garlic- and herb-flavored mashed potatoes.
I've always wanted to try them, but the fresh herbs required for the recipe haven't been available at the local supermarket.
I was lamenting this problem to a friend and she suggested using a soft cheese with garlic and herbs incorporated, like Boursin.
I was able to find the Boursin and this very simple recipe was the result.

In a pot with salted water, boil until tender:
1 pound potatoes, peeled and cut into chunks
Drain the potatoes and mash with:
Buttermilk (add slowly to achieve the desired consistency)
¼ cup Boursin cheese
salt and pepper
parsley flakes

That's all there is to it. They're quick and delicious and
go well with a variety of dishes.

Wild Rice and Mushrooms

Nothing goes with game and fish like wild rice and mushrooms. There are lots of ways to prepare wild rice and mushrooms. This dish can be used as a stuffing or it can be baked in the oven as a side dish.

Preheat oven to 350 degrees.

In a medium skillet, combine and cook until softened:

2 tablespoons butter (preferably unsalted)   **1 cup mushrooms, finely chopped**
½ cup onions, finely chopped   **¼ cup celery, finely chopped**
1 tablespoon garlic, minced

Stir into mixture:

2 cups cooked wild rice
¼ parsley
½ teaspoon thyme
½ teaspoon sage
salt and pepper to taste

Place ingredients in a buttered baking dishand place in oven for about 20 minutes.

Cream of Morel Soup

Cream of Morel Soup

While this recipe is wonderful with morel mushrooms, it would work with any wild mushroom.
It's a great appetizer for any wild-game dinner.

In a large saucepan, heat until the foam subsides:

4 tablespoons of butter

Sauté:

1 pound of morel mushrooms, sliced

   When the mushrooms have exuded their juices and the liquid has reduced to a few tablespoons, add and boil for several minutes:

½ cup of dry white wine

Stir in and simmer for 5 minutes:

4 cups of pheasant stock (or chicken broth)

Puree the soup in a blender, then return it to the saucepan, adding:

½ cup heavy cream

thyme, salt and pepper to taste

Garnish the soup with a few mushrooms.

Cabbage-and-Roasted Garlic Mashed Potatoes

I know what you're thinking—this doesn't sound very appetizing. Think again.
This is one of the most delicious potato dishes I've ever tried.

In a pot of salted water, boil until soft:
> **2 pounds of potatoes, cubed**

In a skillet, combine until lightly browned:
> **2 tablespoons butter**
> **2 large cloves garlic, finely diced**

To the skillet, add and sweat until the cabbage is slightly softened:
> **¼ of a head of white cabbage, finely shredded**

Drain the potatoes and mash with:
> **The cabbage-garlic mixture**
> **Buttermilk (just enough to make the potatoes fluffy)**
> **Salt and pepper**
> **Chopped parsley**

Creamy Mushroom Soup

Have you ever eaten a truly sumptuous cream of mushroom soup at a fine restaurant? This is that kind of soup.
Its rich flavor makes it a perfect starter for any wild-game meal.

Start by removing the stalks from:
> **16 ounces of button mushrooms**

Thin-slice the caps and chop up the stalks. In a saucepan, heat:
> **2 tablespoons of canola oil**
> **2 ½ tablespoons butter**

Add:
> **1 cup of finely chopped shallot**
> **the mushroom stalks and about two-thirds of the sliced caps**

Fry the mushrooms and shallot for a couple of minutes until soft, then reduce heat, cover and sweat the mushrooms for about 5 minutes. Next, stir in:
> **3 tablespoons of flour**
> **3 cups of game bird stock (canned chicken broth will also work)**
> **3 cups of half-and-half**

Bring to a boil, then reduce the heat and simmer for 10 minutes. Let the soup cool slightly. While you're waiting, sauté the rest of the mushroom caps in 2 tablespoons of butter. When the soup has cooled a bit, pour it in a food processor or blender and puree until it's smooth. Pour the soup back into the saucepan, stir in the sautéed mushroom caps and finish with:
> **5 tablespoons of heavy cream**
> **basil**
> **salt and pepper to taste**

Wild Rice Soufflé

I honestly don't know where I got this recipe. Someone emailed it to the office, but the return address was lost and the sender didn't sign his or her name. Despite the fact that "wild rice soufflé" sounds like an oxymoron, we tried it and it was wonderful. Give it a try and I think you'll agree.

Preheat oven to 375 degrees
In a large, non-stick skillet, combine until softened:
> **½ stick butter**
> **1 small onion, finely diced**
> **pinch of rosemary and thyme**

Reduce heat and quickly stir in:
> **1 cup of all-purpose flour**
> **2 cups of wild rice, cooked**
> **2 cups of heavy cream**

Allow mixture to cool slightly. Using an electric mixer, beat until stiff:
> **4 egg whites**

Very quickly and gently fold wild rice mixture into egg whites. Pour soufflé mixture into a loaf-size bread pan and place in oven 90 minutes or until it starts to brown on the top.

Wild Rice

Place in a sauce pan:
> **1 cup uncooked wild rice**
> **1½ cups chicken broth or water**

Cover and simmer over low heat until it "pops" or opens. With this rice, that's usually about 30 minutes. You can add sautéed slivered almonds or mushrooms just before serving.

Wild Rice Soup

Want quick and easy? This recipe takes almost no time to prepare and it's a wonderful starter for any wild-game meal.

In a large saucepan, combine over medium heat:
> **2 cups of cooked wild rice**
> **½ pound of browned and crumbled bacon**
> **1 pound of Velveeta**
> **1 sautéed onion**
> **2 cans of cream of potato soup**
> **1 quart of half and half**
> **10 ounces of sautéed mushrooms.**

Stir frequently until the cheese is melted. That's all there is to it.

Morels and Stuffing

This recipe goes particularly well with fried fish. Since the opening of fishing season coincides with the emergence of morel mushrooms, that makes it a great combination. If you're not a morel-picker, any of the wild mushrooms now available in most grocery stores will work. If wild mushrooms aren't available, button mushrooms will do.

For the stuffing:

Melt 2 tablespoons of butter in a sauté pan and stir in, simmering until softened:

¾ cup onion, finely diced
1 cup celery, finely diced
2 cloves garlic

In a large mixing bowl, combine and mix thoroughly:

5 cups of croutons
1 egg
1 cup of pheasant stock (or chicken broth)
the onion-celery mix
sage, rosemary and thyme to taste (use plenty)

Here's a tip for washing morels or any mushroom. Always rinse the mushrooms in cold water and place them on paper towels. Do not soak the mushrooms in water. Morels are a wet mushrooms and should be kept as dry as possible.

When the croutons have absorbed all the moisture from the stock—you want the stuffing to be quite moist—spoon the stuffing into a buttered casserole dish and place in a 375-degree oven for one hour or until the stuffing is cooked and becoming crispy on top.

For the sauce:

In a sauté pan, melt 1 tablespoon of butter and add:

3 cups of morels (or any mushroom) sliced, rinsed and patted dry

When the mushrooms are cooked and have given off thei juices, stir in:

3 tablespoons heavy cream
2 tablespoons white wine
rosemary, thyme,salt and pepper to taste
1/4 cup pheasant stock (or chicken broth)

Morels and Stuffing, con't.

Allow the sauce to reduce by half, then stir in a very small amount of roux (equal parts melted butter and flour thoroughly mixed over low heat). Very little roux will be required to thicken the sauce. Taste and adjust the seasonings.

Spoon the stuffing onto plates, top with the mushroom sauce and serve with fried fish.

'Squashed' Potatoes

We had this side dish in a restaurant once and liked it so much we started experimenting with ways to make it. It's a very simple recipe that goes well with any wild game but is especially good with venison and duck. The actual preparation time is just minutes, but it's sure to bring "oohs" and "aahs" from your guests. This tasty dish can be prepared ahead of time and reheated in a 350-degree oven for 30 minutes uncovered.

Preheat oven to 350 degrees.
Cut in half and remove the seeds from:

1 butternut squash

Place squash in a glass baking dish, cut-side down, and add 1 inch of water to dish. Add:

5 cloves of garlic, peeled and cut in half.

Place in oven.
Next, peel and slice enough potatoes to equal the weight of the squash. Boil potatoes until done.

When the squash is done, reserve the garlic and remove the meat from the squash, discarding the skin. Drain the potatoes, add the squash and garlic and mash thoroughly, using:

1 stick butter
Salt and pepper to taste

That's all there is to it. Top each serving with a pat of butter and salt and pepper to taste.

Wild Rice-and-Mushroom Risotto

Wild rice-and-mushroom risotto is the perfect accompaniment for just about any wild-game dish. This is a variation of recipes were took from "The Joy of Cooking" and the "Great Chefs" television show. It but really isn't that difficult or complicated to prepare, although it does dirty a lot of pots and pans. But I think you'll agree, it's worth it.

In a medium saucepan over low heat, simmer:
> **4 cups of game stock or chicken broth**

In another medium saucepan, covered, over low heat, combine:
> **1 cup wild rice**
> **2 cups game stock or chicken broth**

In a large, heavy, non-stick skillet over medium heat, melt:
> **2 extra-virgin olive oil**

Add and cook until soft but not browned:
> **1 medium onion, minced**

Increase the heat under the onions slightly and stir in:
> **1 cup of Arborio rice**

Stir the rice with a wooden spoon for about three minutes. Do not allow it to burn. When it begins to look chalky, stir in:
> **½ cup dry white wine**

Once the wine has absorbed, stir in:
> **1 cup of the simmered stock or chicken broth**

Continue to stir until the first cup is absorbed, then add and stir in another cup.

In another skillet, brown in butter:
> **1 cup mushroom, sliced**
> **½ red bell pepper, diced**

Wild Rice-and-Mushroom Risotto, con't.

After the second cup of stock has been absorbed by the rice, stir in:

1 cup of the cooked wild rice
1 cup of stock
the softened mushrooms and pepper

At this point, begin tasting the rice. The grains should be tender but firm rather than mushy. If it's too firm, stir in:

½ cup game stock

Turn off the heat and fold in:

1 tablespoon butter
½ cup grated fresh Parmesan cheese
salt and fresh-ground pepper to taste

Let sit for a few minutes before serving.

Never cover risotto during preparation
It's amazing how much stock the rice can absorb.
Add the final cup a bit at a time. You don't want the rice to become mushy.
If available, get fresh Parmesan and grate it yourself.

Sauces & Marinades

Fish Cakes with Sauce

Lemon-butter Sauce

One of our favorite restaurants has on its appetizer menu crabcakes with lemon-butter sauce. Served with a nice glass of white wine, it's so delicious we sometimes go there just to have an appetizer, skipping the main course. While the chef refused to share his secret with us, we experimented with a variety of recipes until we came up with something just as good. The secret to making this recipe is stirring the butter into the sauce one pat at a time over a low heat. This process is a bit time-consuming, but if you rush the butter, all you'll wind up with is flavored melted butter.

In an enamel or stainless steel saucepan, over medium heat, bring to a boil:

> **½ to ¾ of a fresh, sliced lemon**
> **1 shallot, diced**
> **¼ cup champagne vinegar**

Add and reduce by half:

> **1 cup white wine**
> **1 teaspoon thyme**
> **1 tablespoon fresh parsley**

Add and reduce by half:

> **½ cup heavy cream**

When the cream is reduced, remove from heat and stir in, one pat at a time:

> **1 ½ sticks very cold, unsalted butter**

If the pan gets cool, place it over the edge of the burner (lowest heat) for a few seconds, then remove from heat.

Strain the sauce, and season to taste with:

> **Fresh or dried dill**
> **Salt and pepper**

Pineapple-Basil Sauce

*This sauce goes great with just about any fish dish, but it's particularly good with baked, poached or broiled fish.
Place the fish next to a bed of wild rice and drizzle the sauce over both the rice and the fish. Then sit back and wait for the "ooohs"
and "aaahs" from your guests. Pouring the finished sauce in a cup and placing it in the refrigerator allows the flavors to incorporate.
You can store the sauce for several days, heating in the microwave when it's time to serve.*

In a small stainless steel or enamel saucepan over medium heat, place:
> **½ cup crushed fresh pineapple (canned will work if fresh isn't available)**

Shake the pan until the juices release, then stir in, allowing to reduce by half:
> **¼ cup white wine**

When the wine has reduced, add and bring to boil, stirring vigorously:
> **¾ cup heavy cream**

Remove from heat and stir in, one pat at a time:
> **2 tablespoons unsalted butter**
> **1 tablespoon fresh lemon juice**
> **¼ teaspoon dried basil or 3 leaves chopped fresh basil**

Return to heat briefly, bringing to a final boil. Salt and pepper to taste, pour in a cup
and place in refrigerator. When it's time to serve, heat in a microwave.

Kris' Marinade

Combine in a mixing bowl:
> **½ cup vinegar**
> **2 teaspoons salt**
> **2 cloves garlic**

Pour over meat and refrigerate, covered, overnight

Mustard Butter Sauce

This sauce is a bit time-consuming, but it's worth the effort. It's actually a variation of a white butter sauce called Beurre Blanc in France, where it originated. The trick to making this sauce is incorporating the butter a tablespoon at a time, whisking it constantly after removing the saucepan from the heat. When one pat is nearly melted, add another and stir vigorously until the next is nearly dissolved. Be sure to remove the pan from the heat when stirring in the butter or the butter will separate. An enamel saucepan seems to work best for this recipe. You can strain the sauce before serving or, if you prefer, leave the shallots in the sauce.

Combine in an enamel or thick-walled sauce pan over medium heat, simmering uncovered until it reduced by three-fourths:

6 tablespoons dry white wine
2 tablespoons white wine vinegar
3 tablespoons minced shallots

After the contents have reduced, stir in:

1 ½ tablespoons heavy cream

Remove from heat and whisk in, one tablespoon at a time:

8 tablespoons unsalted butter, cold

If the saucepan cools so the butter won't melt, return the pan to the burner just long enough to warm it up. This is the slow part of the recipe because the butter melts very slowly. It's critical not to rush the process, however, or you'll wind up with melted butter rather than a creamy sauce.

Just before serving, stir in:

½ teaspoon Dijon mustard
½ teaspoon French whole-grain mustard
1 teaspoon fresh lemon juice

Serve immediately.

Barbeque Sauce

In a small sauce pan over medium heat, combine and cook until softened:
> **4 tablespoons butter**
> **2 cloves minced garlic**

Stir in and bring to boil:
> **2 cups ketchup**
> **½ cup water**
> **6 tablespoons brown sugar**
> **½ teaspoon fresh ground pepper**
> **2 tablespoons Worcestershire sauce**
> **1 teaspoon liquid smoke**

Reduce heat and simmer for 5 minutes.

Lemon Butter Sauce

In a stainless steel or enamel saucepan, reduce by half:
> **3 lemon slices**
> **1 diced shallot**
> **¼ cup champagne or wine vinegar**

Add and reduce by half:
> **½ cup heavy cream**

Remove pan to low heat and whisk in, stirring constantly:
> **1 ½ sticks unsalted butter**

Strain the sauce, season to taste with salt and pepper and dill weed.

Serve immediately, or keep in a warm place until its ready to be served.

Mushroom Sauce

In the same skillet used to brown the meat, add:

8 ounces of sliced mushrooms

1 small shallot, chopped

Brown the mushrooms thoroughly, then deglaze the pan with:

1 cup dry white wine

When the wine has nearly evaporated, stir in:

½ cup gamebird stock (or chicken broth)

½ cup heavy cream

Allow the sauce to reduce for a few minutes, then stir in:

Enough roux to thicken slightly

To finish the sauce, turn off the heat and stir in:

2 tablespoons butter

salt and pepper to taste

Lemon-Dill Sauce

Of all the lemon sauce recipes listed in this cookbook, this is my favorite.

In a small saucepan over medium-high heat, combine and reduce by three-fourths:

6 tablespoons white white

2 tablespoons white wine vinegar

3 tablespoons chopped shallots

When the wine has reduced, stir in:

1 tablespoon heavy white cream

1 tablespoon lemon zest (grated lemon peel)

salt and pepper

dill weed to taste

When thoroughly combined, remove from heat and stir in:

8 tablespoons unsalted butter

Mushroom-Port Sauce

This recipe got rave reviews from everyone who tried it.

In a sauté pan over medium-high heat, combine:
>**2 tablespoons of finely diced shallots**
>**6 ounces of sliced mushrooms**

When the mushrooms and shallots are softened, de-glaze the pan with:
>**¼ cup Port**
>**¼ cup of stock**

When the port-stock mixture has reduced until it's sticky, add and boil down quickly:
>**1 cup heavy cream**

When the sauce begins to thicken, turn off the heat and add:
>**A squirt of lemon juice**
>**½ tablespoon dried parsley flakes**
>**salt and pepper to taste**

Pour the sauce over gamebird pieces.

Plum Dandy Port Sauce

This wonderful sauce works well with any dark-meat game. It can be poured over duck, goose or venison.
Best of all, it's relatively easy to prepare.

In a saucepan, bring to a simmer:
> **2 cups of Port**

Add and cook for 15 minutes over medium heat:
> **½ cup orange juice**
> **1 tablespoon lemon juice**

Stir in and reduce by half over medium-low heat:
> **1 ½ cups venison stock (or beef broth)**
> **1 clove of garlic, crushed**
> **½ teaspoon of Worcestershire sauce**
> **1 tablespoon Oriental plum sauce**
> **1 shallot, diced**

Strain and continue to cook until the sauce thickens. Before serving, whisk in, one pat at a time:
> **4 tablespoons of unsalted butter, cold**

Before serving, season with:
> **Salt and pepper**
> **Parsley**

Sweet, Simple Orange Sauces

Nothing enhances the flavor of roast duck or goose like a good orange sauce. Take a fat, juicy mallard or Canada goose—preferably braised—and brown the skin until it's crispy. Then pour a rich orange sauce over the top and you've got the makings of a wonderful meal.

Some of the following recipes call for duck stock. If you don't have any, chicken broth will work.

To prepare my favorite sauce, combine in a saucepan over medium heat:
> **½ cup frozen orange juice (concentrate)**
> **1 tablespoon fresh minced ginger**
> **2 tablespoons Grand Marnier**
> **1 tablespoon soy sauce**
> **¼ cup duck stock (or chicken broth)**

Reduce until the mixture becomes syrupy, then add:
> **2 tablespoons brown sugar**
> **2 tablespoons current jelly**

Off heat and finish by stirring in:
> **Salt and pepper to taste**
> **2 tablespoons of butter**

Another great recipe begins by combining in a saucepan over medium heat:
> **2 tablespoons balsamic vinegar**
> **1 tablespoon fresh grated ginger**
> **1 cup fresh-squeezed orange juice**

Reduce by half and add:
> **1 cup of duck stock**

Reduce by half and finish with:
> **3 tablespoons Grand Marnier**
> **salt and pepper to taste**

Sweet, Simple Orange Sauces, cont.

Here's another easy one. Over medium heat, reduce by half:

½ cup fresh-squeezed orange juice

Add and reduce by half:

1 cup duck stock

Finish by stirring in:

2 tablespoons Grand Marnier

2 tablespoons butter

The quickest recipe I've found calls for combining:

½ cup orange marmalade

3 tablespoons Grand Marnier

2 tablespoons soy sauce

1 tablespoon fresh grated ginger

2 tablespoons current jelly

Cook over medium heat until the mixture becomes syrupy. This last recipe is a bit sweet for my taste but some readers may find it to their liking.

Minnesota Marinade

Apparently this recipe for a venison marinade has been bouncing around Minnesota longer than some of our favorite Ole and Lena jokes. We received it from several different sources. Official credit goes to Curt Johnson of the Minnesota Department of Tourism who says he got it from Todd McDonald of the Minnesota News Network as supplied to him by Minneapolis Tribune outdoor writer Ron Schara. See what I mean? And that's only one of several contributors who submitted it. Anyway, here's the recipe:

In a large mixing bowl, combine and blend well:

½ cup of cooking oil	**2 tablespoons of soy sauce**
1 teaspoon Worcestershire sauce	**¼ teaspoon dry mustard**
½ cup wine (red or white)	**½ cup ketchup**
3 small cloves of garlic	**1 teaspoon lemon juice**

Pour over venison and let stand 3 hours at room temperature. Cook meat on grill.

Bob Mitchell's Venison Marinade

Bob Mitchell is a long-time friend of our company. Bob works for Campbell Ewald, the Detroit-based advertising that handles Chevy Trucks. He's an avid fisherman who has joined us on a number of Canadian outings, a rabid duck hunter who spends lots of time on Lake St. Clair and—based on the recipe he sent along—likes to hunt deer as well.

Combine in a large mixing bowl:

3 cups of oil
1 cup soy sauce
1 cup honey
8 tablespoons green onions, tops and all
4 cloves of garlic
8 tablespoons of vinegar
6 teaspoons of dried ginger

Pour the marinade over a batch of venison steaks and refrigerate for 8 hours.
Grill to medium-rare, turning 3 to 4 times.

Honey-Mustard Dipping Sauce

This sauce goes great with fried or deep-fried appetizers like venison chislic, pheasant fingers or pheasant strips.
It takes seconds to prepare and can be as spicy or as mild as you like.

In a small mixing bowl, combine:
> **4 tablespoons of honey**
> **¼ cup Dijon mustard**
> **1 tablespoon dill weed**
> **Cajun seasoning to taste (optional)**

Before serving, taste the sauce and adjust the seasonings to taste. To add zing to this recipe, add some horseradish.

Mushroom-cream sauce

In a small saute pan, combine and brown:
> **3 tablespoons butter**
> **1 cup chopped mushrooms**

When the mushrooms are browned, pour in:
> **¼ cup white wine**

Allow the wine to reduce. When it's almost gone, pour in:
> **½ cup fish stock**

Allow stock to reduce slightly, then add:
> **¼ cup heavy cream**

Bring to a boil and thicken by stirring in small amounts of roux.

Index

Index

Index